THE VICTORIOUS TEEN

Buddhist Advice for Dealing With What Life Throws at You

DAISAKU IKEDA

Illustrated by Tim Paul

World Tribune
Press

Published by World Tribune Press
A division of the SGI-USA
606 Wilshire Blvd.
Santa Monica, CA 90401

Illustrations: Tim Paul, www.timpaulillustrations.com © 2016
Cover and Interior Design: SunDried Penguin

10 9 8 7 6 5 4 3 2

ISBN: 978-1-935523-73-4

Library of Congress Control Number: 2015931002

Contents

You & Others

YoU & the World

Editor's Note

Daisaku Ikeda has spent a lifetime encouraging young people. Through countless written works—speeches, essays, dialogues—the SGI leader has urged young people to believe in themselves, dream big, and lead noble lives dedicated to serving others.

The editors at World Tribune Press have compiled excerpts of SGI President Ikeda's guidance from numerous sources and formatted them here in a way to make them accessible and relevant for teens. We also added inspirational quotes from Nichiren's writings and from famous individuals the SGI leader himself has quoted over the years.

We hope that this collection of advice will help young people everywhere find answers they're looking for so they can build a foundation of faith that will last throughout their lives.

The citations most commonly used in this book have been abbreviated as follows:

GZ, page number(s) refers to the *Gosho zenshu*, the Japanese-language compilation of letters, treatises, essays, and oral teachings of Nichiren Daishonin.

OTT, page number(s) refers to *The Record of the Orally Transmitted Teachings*, translated by Burton Watson (Tokyo: Soka Gakkai, 2004).

WND, page number(s) refers to *The Writings of Nichiren Daishonin*, vol. 1 (WND-1) (Tokyo: Soka Gakkai, 1999) or vol. 2 (WND-2) (Tokyo: Soka Gakkai, 2006).

YOU

Hope is the greatest weapon in the world.

—**Daisaku Ikeda**

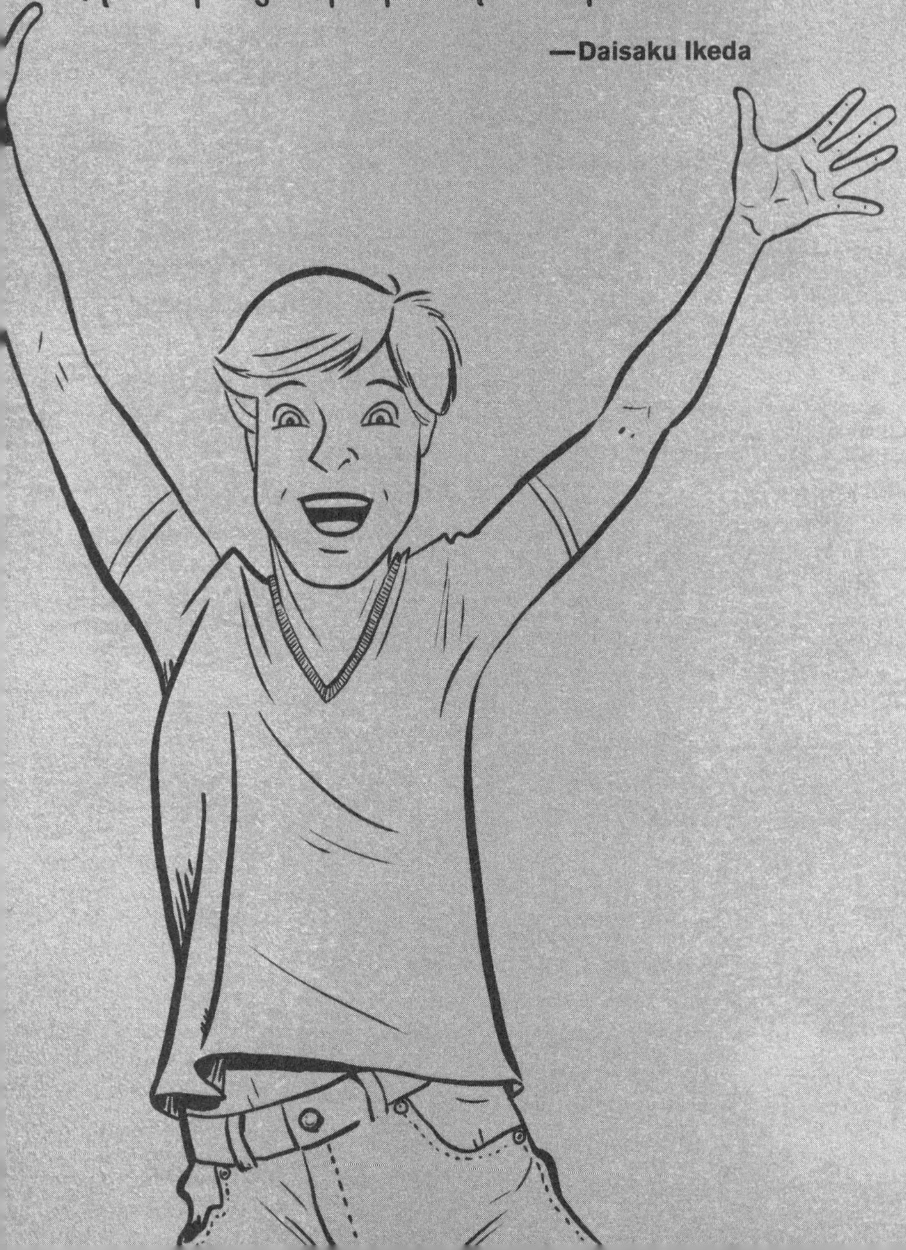

How to
Believe in Yourself

Believe in Yourself

My mentor, Josei Toda, would often say, "When you are young, it is very important to believe in yourself." And: "It is essential for young people to have something they can truly believe in. They need to trust their own hearts." The purpose of faith is to make our hearts strong and steadfast, to develop inner strength and conviction. Everything depends on our minds and our hearts. The ultimate conclusion of Nichiren Buddhism is summed up in the words, "It is the heart that is important" (WND-1, 1000).

Don't Believe in the Negative Comments of Others

It is so important for you young people not to be defeated by your environment. You mustn't lose faith in yourself. Each of you has a mission in this lifetime that only you can fulfill. Each of you has a life that only you can live and from which you can create something of value. Whatever else you may doubt, I hope you will never doubt this.

Even should someone look upon you as a lost cause, you must never look upon yourself that way. Should others berate you as having no talent or ability, you mustn't succumb to the negative message of their words. Unperturbed by anyone's negativity, grit your teeth, keep believing in yourself, chant Nam-myoho-renge-kyo, and face your challenges with all your might.

Don't Give Up on Yourself

Many of history's most famous people seemed far from outstanding in their youth. Winston Churchill (1874–1965) was known for always failing at school. Mahatma Gandhi (1869–1948) wasn't a remarkable student either; he was shy, timid, and a poor speaker. Albert Einstein (1879–1955), also, was a mediocre student, but luckily he excelled in math. And Wilhelm Roentgen (1845–1923), the discoverer of X-rays, was expelled from his polytechnic school when classmates falsely accused him of causing an accident. So what did these four young men have in common? Their refusal to give up on themselves.

It makes no difference if the practitioner himself is lacking in worth, defective in wisdom, impure in his person, and lacking in virtue derived from observing the precepts. So long as he chants Nam-myoho-renge-kyo, [the Buddhist gods] will invariably protect him. One does not throw away gold because the bag that holds it is dirty.

—Nichiren

How to Be
Someone Who Never Gives Up

Resolve Not to Be Defeated in the Future

In life, of course, there are times when we are unable to win. There may also be times when it seems that we will be crushed by adversity. But even at such moments, we must never allow ourselves to be beaten in our hearts. We must resolve not to be defeated in the future. We practice Nichiren Buddhism so that we can be victorious in life.

Don't concern yourself with vanity or pretension. Just earnestly continue to chant Nam-myoho-renge-kyo. That will rouse strong life force, and brighten your face too. Just like a jet taking off, your life state will begin to rise rapidly, because chanting revs up the engine of your life until it's running at full speed. Always aim for the top, win over yourself, and create a proud record of triumph for all the world to see. That's the way to enjoy an invigorating and fulfilling life.

> Keep your face always toward the sunshine—
> and shadows fall behind you.

Walt Whitman
1819–1992
Poet, Essayist, Journalist

There Is No Need to Worry

When we have problems, there is no need to fret or worry. Problems can make us a better and stronger person. The German writer Johann Wolfgang von Goethe (1749–1832) imparted the message that fortune smiles on those who persist with courage and integrity.[1] When you come up against a difficulty, don't give in to defeat or despair. Stand tall and proudly forge ahead on the path of your mission. If you do, you will eventually be able to transform poison into medicine and usher in a brilliant new day.

I Get Really Dejected by Failures or Disappointments

That is precisely when you need to make a conscious effort to be strong and positive. We are most vulnerable to negativity when we are discouraged and filled with self-doubt. If you face such times by chanting Nam-myoho-renge-kyo vibrantly and challenging such negativity head-on, you can dispel it.

Become the master of your mind rather than let your mind master you.

—Nichiren

How to Stop Worrying About
What Others Think of You

You Know Yourself Best

Each of you knows yourself best. The opinions or evaluations of others may be based on emotion or ill intention. You can never tell. That's why it's important to view yourselves continually through the eyes of Buddhism, pondering from time to time, "Am I living a respectable life?"

Don't Live in Fear of Being Judged—Be Brave Instead

When we're afraid of being laughed at, of embarrassment, of being looked down on by others for our mistakes, shortcomings, or limitations, progress becomes very difficult. We must be brave. So what if others laugh? Whoever makes fun of those trying their best are the ones who should be ashamed.

PHOTO: HULTON ARCHIVE/GETTY IMAGES

You gain strength, courage, and confidence by every experience in which you really stop to look fear in the face…. You must do the thing you think you cannot do.

Eleanor Roosevelt
1884–1962
Diplomat, U.S. First Lady, Peace and Human Rights Activist

How Do I Stop Worrying About What Other People Think of Me?

Perhaps you've heard of the first lady Eleanor Roosevelt (1884–1962), who remains one of the most respected women in the United States. She once wrote: "Looking back, I see how abnormally timid and shy I was as a girl. As long as I let timidity and shyness dominate me I was half paralyzed."[2]

Through self-discipline, Mrs. Roosevelt conquered her fear. What concrete measures did she take? Like most shy people, she was plagued by fears about herself, so she applied herself earnestly to break those chains. First, she stopped worrying about making a good impression on others and caring what they thought of her. Rather than thinking only about herself, she began thinking of the well-being of others. Second, she pursued wholeheartedly that which interested her and exerted herself to accomplish what she chose to accomplish. She learned that people don't pay much attention to what others are doing and that the amount of attention we pay ourselves is actually our greatest enemy. Realizing this, Mrs. Roosevelt put great effort toward disregarding herself. Third, her sense of adventure and desire to experience life were helpful in overcoming her shyness. She maintained a lively spirit to discover what life had to offer.[3]

By continuing to challenge herself, Mrs. Roosevelt gradually gained confidence. She was later involved in historic initiatives, such as the drafting of the United Nations' Universal Declaration of Human Rights. And she was loved by many people.

How to
Not compare Yourself to others

Be True to Yourself

I cannot say this too strongly: Do not compare yourselves to others. Be true to who you are, and continue to learn with all your might. Even if you are ridiculed, even if you suffer disappointments and setbacks, continue to advance and do not be defeated. If you have such a strong determination in your heart, you are already halfway to victory.

When you hold fast to your beliefs and live true to yourself, your true value as a human being shines through. Buddhism teaches the concept of manifesting one's true nature. This means to reveal your genuine innate self, your true inherent potential, and bring it to shine, illuminating all around you. It refers to your most refined individuality and uniqueness.

Comparing Yourself to Others Can Be Depressing

In the writing "On Attaining Buddhahood in This Lifetime," Nichiren states, "It is like spending night and day counting one's neighbor's wealth but gaining not even half a coin" (see WND-1, 3). Nichiren uses this metaphor to explain that it is pointless for us to seek enlightenment outside our own life.

Instead of comparing yourself to others and becoming depressed, adopt a positive attitude and take others' example as inspiration and motivation to improve yourself.

Even Mr. Toda, who was so self-confident and outgoing, told me that he had to work hard to overcome the feelings of inferiority that plagued him when he was young.

Being able to recognize others' strong points is in itself a very admirable quality. The next step is to recognize your own strong points and develop them to the fullest.

Compare Yourself to…Yourself

It's not important how you compare yourself to others but how you compare yourself to whom you were yesterday. If you see that you've advanced even one step, then you've achieved a victory.

You Have a Unique Purpose

The fact that we have been born into this world means that we each have a unique purpose to fulfill. If we didn't, we would not have been born. Nothing in the universe is without value. Everything has meaning. Even plants that we spurn as weeds have a function. Each living thing has a unique identity, role, and purpose—the cherry as a cherry, the plum as a plum, the peach as a peach, the damson as a damson.

There's no point in a plum trying to be a cherry. The plum should bloom like a plum, revealing its unique potential to the fullest. Not only does doing so accord with reason, but it is the right path to happiness and fulfillment in life. Each of us has a distinct identity—that's what makes life interesting. How dull things would be if we were all alike!

> To be yourself in a world that is constantly trying to make you something else is the greatest accomplishment.

Ralph Waldo Emerson
1803–82
Essayist, Lecturer, Poet

How to
Build Self-confidence

How Do I Build Self-Confidence?

Self-confidence comes from hard work and effort. You're deluding yourself if you think you can have self-confidence without it. Only those who strive to challenge a goal and work toward it at their own pace and in their own way, only those who keep trying, no matter how many times they may fail, can develop unshakable confidence in themselves. Self-confidence is synonymous with an invincible will. You cannot be said to have true self-confidence if your opinion of yourself seesaws from high to low every time you compare yourself to others. A life spent judging yourself in terms of others will only end in frustration and deadlock.

Even a feeble person will not stumble if those supporting him are strong, but a person of considerable strength, when alone, may fall down on an uneven path.

—Nichiren

If You Really Believe You Can Do Something, You Can

The British essayist William Hazlitt (1778–1830) was an acute observer of human psychology. He wrote that if we believe we can win, we can, asserting that confidence is a prerequisite for victory. The belief that you will win without fail summons all your strength, even that which is normally latent, and makes your triumph a reality.

The human brain has been called a microcosm. Some believe that billions of nerve cells can be found in the brain. When all their interrelated combinations are taken into account, the number becomes astronomical.

The potential of the human brain remains an unknown. We do not know what powers it holds.

But one thing is certain: The power of belief, the power of thought, will move reality in the direction of what we believe and how we conceive it. If you really believe you can do something, you can. That is a fact.

When you clearly envision a victorious outcome, engrave it in your heart, and are firmly convinced that you will attain it, your brain makes every effort to realize the mental image you have created. Then, through your unceasing efforts, that victory is finally made a reality.

If you really believe you can do something, you can. That is a fact. (PHOTO: DAIGO OTOBE)

How to
Defeat Insecurities

I'm Just Starting at a New School, and I Feel Nervous About It

Everyone is anxious and insecure in a new environment. It's quite natural.

You're not alone. Everyone is anxious or worried—that's how it is. Even your friends who appear confident have some kind of problem of their own. It's human to have problems. You're all human beings. You're all junior high students. It's natural to feel anxious. There's nothing wrong with being anxious, but it's wrong to let it defeat you.

I Am Short, and People at School Make Fun of Me. I Feel Insecure and Self-Conscious. How Should I Deal With This?

Complexes about physical appearance—thinking you're too short or too fat or have a terrible complexion or are unattractive—cause the most intense suffering and are the hardest to talk to others about.

When you succumb to a complex, you are likely to see everything about yourself in a negative light. When something doesn't work out for you, you tend to blame it on those things that make you feel inferior: "It's because I'm short" and so forth. When you adopt this negative attitude, you close your heart to the wonderful potential you possess and negate your good points as well, which only insures that things keep going from bad to worse in your life.

When your feelings of inferiority are really strong, you think everyone is laughing at you. The truth is that people are not nearly as interested in you as you imagine.

Self-consciousness is so much a part of being young that it probably doesn't do any good to say, "Don't be self-conscious." The important thing is to accept the fact that you are self-conscious, that you have a complex, but not let those feelings of inferiority beat you. You can use those feelings as a springboard to maximize your strong points.

Use Your Insecurities as a Means to Improve Yourself

If you feel self-conscious about being short, then just go ahead and feel as self-conscious as you want! But it's silly to think that being short means you're worthless or no good. You can say to yourself: "I may be short, but I'm going to have the biggest heart possible!" "I may be short, but I am going to be the best student in my school!" "I know how it feels to be teased, so I will never tease anyone!" "I'm going to be a person who is kind and considerate!"

These are some of the ways you can use your complex as a spur to growth and self-improvement. You mustn't let it defeat you. That's the key.

A complex, if you win over it, can become a means for forging strength and confidence. It can become a plus for you. Your worries about your complex, your experiences of being picked on by others—all these things enable you to become a deeper, more sensitive person; they help you understand others' feelings. Those who've never had a complex can't appreciate the sensitivity of people's hearts. Mr. Toda said: "Far stronger are those with a sense of inferiority! They are determined to win."

> Don't wait for anyone to deputize you or authorize you or empower you. You have to just start out with yourself… and put one foot in front of the other.

Hazel Henderson
1933–
Futurist, Evolutionary Economist

How to Learn to
Like Yourself, Just as You Are

I Am Quiet by Nature, but I Wish I Were More Talkative. How Can I Become So?

If you are not talkative, how about becoming an excellent listener? You can say to others: "Please tell me about yourself. I want to hear all about you." If you try to make people think you're something that you're not, then speaking will be nothing but torture. You are fine just the way you are. You should let people get to know the real you, including your strengths and weaknesses.

Some people just ramble on mindlessly without saying anything. A person of few words is likely to have far more substance and depth than those who talk just to hear their own voice! Someone who takes action swiftly and effectively is a great deal more trustworthy than someone who is all talk.

Of far greater importance than whether one is quiet or talkative is whether one possesses rich inner substance. The beautiful smile or small, unconscious gesture of a person who, even though reticent, possesses a rich heart, will speak more eloquently than any words. And often such people will speak out with authority and confidence at a crucial moment.

In Buddhism, we say the voice does the Buddha's work. Fundamentally, this refers to chanting Nam-myoho-renge-kyo. Those who chant Nam-myoho-renge-kyo are, in essence, the most eloquent of all. Start with expressing whatever you want to the Gohonzon while chanting. It's important to pray for others' happiness as well. Then, quite naturally, you'll develop the ability to freely and confidently say what you want to say.

I See Only My Faults

People who are strict with themselves often feel that way—it's a sign of a sincere and admirable character.

It's difficult to see ourselves objectively. Nichiren writes, "We ordinary people can see neither our own eyelashes, which are so close, nor the heavens in the distance" (WND-1, 1137). Perhaps you could ask someone who knows you well, like a friend, parent, or sibling, what strong points he or she thinks you have and should develop. I'm sure that person will name many admirable qualities.

No one has only faults or only merits. We all have a mixture of both. Therefore, we should strive to develop and polish our positive attributes. As we do, our shortcomings will fade until they are no longer apparent.

Also, if someone should point out our faults, rather than getting offended or upset, it is to our benefit to listen calmly and objectively to what that person has to say and regard it as constructive criticism. Once you take your place in society, few will be so honest with you.

Exert yourself in the two ways of practice and study. Without practice and study, there can be no Buddhism. You must not only persevere yourself; you must also teach others. Both practice and study arise from faith. Teach others to the best of your ability, even if it is only a single sentence or phrase.

—Nichiren

Sometimes I Lose My Cool and Can Be Passionate and Overly Emotional. It's Embarrassing!

In this unfeeling age, being a bit emotional might not be such a bad thing! You are young, so it's natural to have passionate feelings.

Getting along well with others is of course important, but doing so to the point of suppressing your individuality will only bring you misery. Furthermore, a strong character is almost a requirement to survive in this tumultuous, ever-changing world. And having intense emotions enables you to understand the feelings of others. It is not bad to be passionate, but if it is driven by egotism and hurts others, it can be dangerous. A race car that can reach hundreds of miles an hour also needs extremely powerful brakes.

The point is to develop self-control. And that comes from chanting Nam-myoho-renge-kyo and developing a strong life force. When you bring forth your innate Buddhahood, your passionate nature will become an impetus for progress, a strong sense of justice, and a burning desire to help other people.

I Get Easily Discouraged, and My Resolve Weakens as a Result. How Can I Change This?

Anyone who has ever made a resolution discovers that the strength of that determination fades with time. The moment you feel that is when you should make a fresh determination. Tell yourselves: "OK! I will start again from now!" There is a saying that if you fall down seven times, get up an eighth. Don't give up when you feel discouraged—just pick yourselves up and renew your determination each time.

The important thing is not that our resolve never wavers, but that we don't get down on ourselves or throw in the towel when it does. The fact that we realize we've become lazy is evidence we are growing.

How to
Be Truly Free

Sometimes I Think It Would Be Easier to Just Run Away From My Responsibilities

You can run away, of course. That freedom exists. But it is a very small, petty freedom. It leads only to a life of great hardship, a life in which you are powerless, weak, and completely frustrated. Alongside this small freedom, however, exists a much greater freedom. The well-known Japanese novelist Eiji Yoshikawa (1892–1962) writes, "Great character is forged through hardship." Only by polishing yourself through repeated difficulties can you build a self that sparkles as brightly as a gem. Once you have developed such a state of life, nothing will faze you. You will be free. You will be victorious.

Once you realize this truth, even hardships become enjoyable.

Daring to take on tough challenges—that in itself is immense freedom.

The sea and its waves make it possible for ships to sail from one place to another. Air resistance produces the lift that makes it possible for planes to fly through the sky. Hunger makes food delicious.

Freedom is a relative thing. It is impossible to have absolutely everything go our way all the time. In fact, if it weren't for the various restrictions and obstacles life presents to us, we probably wouldn't appreciate what it is to be free. After all, planes cannot fly in a vacuum; they need air resistance to stay aloft. On the flip side, if we didn't seek freedom, we wouldn't know what it means not to be free.

Face Your Troubles

You may run away from hard work and effort, declaring yourself a free spirit, but you cannot run away from yourself—from your weaknesses, personality, and destiny. It is like trying to run from your shadow. It is even more impossible to escape from the sufferings of birth, aging, sickness, and death inherent in the human condition. The more you try to avoid hardships, the more doggedly they pursue you, like so many relentless hounds nipping at your heels. That's why there is no other way than to turn and face your troubles head-on.

Life is a battle to win ultimate and unlimited freedom. Faith in Buddhism allows us to use our karma and the sufferings of birth, aging, sickness, and death as springboards to happiness. The purpose of faith is to forge that kind of self. Faith enables us to attain a state of unsurpassed freedom.

Free Time Does Not Equal Freedom

Freedom cannot be measured in terms of time—the amount of "free time" we have has nothing to do with the amount of "freedom" we have. It's what we do with our time that counts. Two people with the exact same amount of free time will use it differently: One might savor it, while the other might complain, finding it either burdensome or too short. Similarly, you can spend the same hour watching television, the time passing by in a flash without anything to show for it, or studying, feeling a satisfying sense of achievement when you finish. That one hour can be a turning point in your life. Freedom is determined by your values, by what you place importance on in life.

How to
Bring Out Your Best

Push Yourself

It's important to get in the habit of pushing yourselves an extra five minutes. When you think: "I cannot do anymore; I want to go out and have some fun," that is the time to challenge yourselves to keep at it another five minutes. Those who persevere for an extra five minutes are truly admirable. Victory is theirs. This is one of life's truths.

How to Be Great Instead of Ordinary

Mr. Toda taught us the following about the difference between great lives and ordinary lives. Why weren't the great defeated by their sufferings and temptations?

According to Mr. Toda: "The reason is that their aspirations were not motivated by selfish desires or egocentric concerns. The basis of their aspirations was a desire for the happiness of all humankind, and that gave them great determination."

Their hopes were not petty or short-sighted ambitions. They had faith and philosophy that made them strive for the sake of humanity and the future.

They were convinced that a defeat on their part was not simply a personal defeat but a loss for humanity. That's why they could not permit themselves to lose. They could only win.

Their great hope became the source of an invincible fighting spirit.

Dedicate Yourself to Clear and Lofty Goals

A youth that is spent dedicated to clearly defined and lofty goals—the perfection of the self, contributing to society, making those around one happy, and working for peace—is a beautiful youth. The difference between those who have such clear-cut goals and those who spend their youth in aimless pleasure seeking will become abundantly clear when the time comes to bring their life to its completion.

This lifetime is precious. You are all noble and valuable. I don't want you to spend your youth in a way that will cause you to have regrets or that will cast shadows over your heart in the future. Please live your youth so that you can say at the very end of your life: "I was happy; I was truly fulfilled." May you be able to smile and declare: "I have won!"

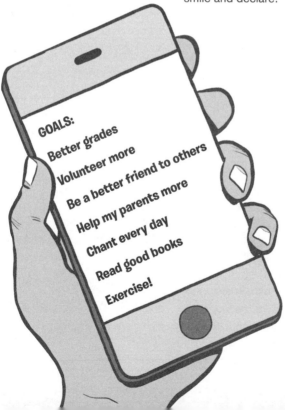

How to
Live the Best Life Possible

What Is the Best Way to Live?

There are lives ruled by envy and jealousy, and lives filled with gloom and ceaseless worry. There are lives consumed with maligning others, lives of ill will bent on bringing others down. There are lives mired in a morass of self-inflicted suffering. Then again, there are lives filled with appreciation and praise for others, lives dedicated to bringing people together. There are honorable lives overflowing with sincere respect for others and committed to helping others become happy. There are lives abounding with victory after victory. We can see all kinds of lives in the human world. Buddhism reveals the best and the most correct way to live. Through Buddhist practice, we can lead lives of supreme value. That is the proof of Buddhism's greatness.

Be Good at Finding Beauty in Life

A truly beautiful person is one who is adept at finding beauty. By beauty I don't mean some elevated, idealized quality. Truly happy are those who find their own distinct excitement and emotion in the course of daily life—being moved by nature's beauty to exclaim: "Look at that beautiful sky! What a lovely sunset! Do you see that flower?" Their lives are rich.

In human relations, too, we can respond in a way that is sensitive to the feelings of others. If we find someone worrying about something, we go to offer our help without a second thought. In my opinion, a person who is sensitive and receptive to feelings, to beauty, is a truly beautiful person.

How to
Face Problems Like a Champion

No Matter What, Keep Moving Forward and Never Give Up

You may encounter situations or events that bring great sadness and despair—such as problems with friends, heartache over love, being involved in a car accident, or having a parent fall ill. But when you look back on such hardships later, they will all seem like a dream.

After World War II, I was in a state of despair. I literally didn't know if I would survive, and the future looked very bleak. But I pushed on and here I am today. Even those difficult times now seem as unreal as if they had never happened.

No matter what hardships we face, if we keep moving forward without giving up, they will all eventually vanish like a mirage. This is an important premise on which to base our lives. So we must live optimistically.

Facing Our Problems Results in Joy

Naturally, everyone wants to avoid problems and unnecessary suffering. No one chooses to worry or suffer. But does the mere absence of hardships or problems equal happiness? No, the true essence of happiness is inner fulfillment. And the way to attain a true sense of fulfillment is to face our problems, work hard to solve them, and triumph over them. Everyone has experienced, to a greater or lesser degree, the joy this process brings.

Overcoming Obstacles

There are many obstacles we encounter in the course of life. One issue after another presents itself. But Buddhism teaches that earthly desires lead to enlightenment, and each time we conquer a problem we reach a higher and more expansive spiritual state.

We must face each issue that crops up, without flinching, solve it, overcome it, and move on to the next. That is what human life is really about. That is what it is to be alive. When you triumph over your sufferings, they will all be transformed into joy. And you yourself will grow and expand.

The Most Direct Route to Victory

When facing a series of difficult challenges, the way to break through them is to keep forging bravely straight ahead. That is the quickest and most direct route to victory.

There may be times when you come to a temporary standstill, feeling too discouraged or exhausted to continue. When that happens, just take a deep breath and set out anew once more when you feel ready. Remember, we are always together, traveling on a shared journey.

Given that struggles and challenges are an unavoidable part of life, we might as well make our way with a joyful, positive spirit. That has been my attitude. No matter what criticism or abuse was directed at me, I never retreated a single step. This is because I am the disciple of the lionhearted Josei Toda.

Nichiren's disciples cannot accomplish anything if they are cowardly.

—Nichiren

How to
Develop Inner Strength

Be a Person of Conviction

A cowardly person will undermine even the hearts and minds of others. A person of conviction, on the other hand, beholds vast expanses of creativity stretching before them.

Those who live their youth and their lives with conviction will not waver in the least, no matter what difficulties arise. Here is found the essence of being human. Nothing can match a person of conviction. Such a person can crown his or her life with victory.

"The tougher the going gets, the stronger I will become, the more value I will create"—this is the spirit of a true lion of Soka. I want all of you, as such courageous young men and women, to strive to become first-rate people who are considered as authorities in your chosen fields. Please work hard, persevere, and attain victory. By winning, you will make your parents happy. Your teachers will be delighted, and I will rejoice. And you, too, will also be happy.

The Ultimate Way of Life

Faith is not for anyone but yourself—it is all for you. Working to spread Nichiren's teachings, devoting yourself to chanting Nam-myoho-renge-kyo, and studying Nichiren's writings and Buddhist theory while you are young are all tasks that transform your life into a garden of blessings and merits.

Society is full of contradictions. Many times, our lives are upset by the inexorable workings of past karma. All existence is nothing but change, a succession of changes. Flowers fall, and joyful times pass quickly. Nothing stays the same.

In this existence, where all life is constantly in a state of flux, how do we obtain unshakable happiness? To live in the actual world of everyday reality while believing in the great, unchanging, eternal Law of Nam-myoho-renge-kyo—this is what constitutes the ultimate way of life. If you make the Mystic Law the basis of your existence, you will be able to rise above any difficulties in life. You will be able to transform harsh karma. You will be able to convert worries, tears, and sufferings into the fuel, the sustenance, for growth and victory.

And as you repeat that process, you will without a doubt build a life of genuine happiness. Faith is not some kind of duty. It is a right you have, a right you can exercise to attain happiness.

It is crucial that you obtain your own happiness, and you cannot do that in a life of only ease and comfort. You can only attain happiness in the battle against the buffeting wind and waves. That is why the road to happiness will never be opened to you unless you are strong, as strong as you can be.

SGI President Ikeda encourages an elementary school student during a future division course on the Soka University campus in Hachioji, Tokyo, August 1975. (PHOTO: SEIKYO PRESS)

How to Be
Truly Happy... No Matter What

Happiness Is Something You Have to Build for Yourself

Please do not allow yourself to become a shallow person, enraptured by and envious of glamour and stylish appearances. Those who are too easily moved by the glittering surface of things have not established their own firm core or self-identity. They lack a philosophy of life, their own beliefs, and they have no standards to live by. They just float along, and their lives are aimless and undirected.

The purpose of life is to attain happiness. Happiness is something that you feel inside. It is something you have to build for yourself. It is something that lives within you. That is why the state of your own inner realm, your life, is so crucial to being happy. Happiness is not in some far-off place. Happiness exists within your own life, within a single thought in your mind. You yourself are the most noble and precious of all. You have no need to be envious of anyone or to long for things far away.

Faith and one's single-minded desire to achieve kosen-rufu are what makes this "self" of yours shine its brightest and develop to its greatest potential; they are what fill you with good fortune, satisfaction, and eternal joy. This is the essence of true happiness. A palace exists within your own life. When you open that palace, you can be happy wherever you are.

Realize That Everything Can Be Transformed Into a Source of Happiness

An absence of suffering does not equal happiness. Happiness depends on developing the state of mind where one is able to transform all sufferings into joy. This rigorous struggle in turn gives rise to immense satisfaction and value. The greater hardships one undergoes, the greater potential that exists for one to grow. The deeper one's suffering, the more profound will be the joy one experiences when one triumphs over it. Difficulties lead to enlightenment, great obstacles lead to Buddhahood.

It would be lovely not to have to encounter any hardships, but just as exams give an impetus to one's studies, without hardships there can be no progress or growth. Ultimately, when we live in accord with the great eternal Law, everything in our lives becomes a source of happiness. Without this firm basis, any happiness, no matter how wonderful it may appear, is but transitory and fleeting.

No pessimist ever discovered the secret of the stars, or sailed to an uncharted land, or opened a new doorway for the human spirit.

Helen Keller
1880–1968
Author, Activist, Lecturer

How to
Not Be a Lazy Procrastinator

I Can Be Lazy, Especially When Faced With Something Difficult. How Can I Become More Motivated?

I think half the problem's already solved, because you know what the problem is!

People tend to lack willpower. To take the path of least resistance is human nature. Outstanding individuals didn't become great overnight. They disciplined themselves to overcome their weaknesses, conquering apathy and inertia to become true victors in life.

Life is a struggle with ourselves. It is a tug-of-war between moving forward and regressing, between happiness and unhappiness. Those short on willpower or self-motivation should chant Nam-myoho-renge-kyo with conviction to become people of strong will, who can tackle any problem with real seriousness and determination.

Time Management— Use Your Time Wisely

Nichiren Daishonin writes that one day of life is more valuable than all the treasures of the universe (see WND-1, 955).

Time equals life. It is a priceless treasure. Those who value time, value life. Those who value life are the ones who will create peace in the world. The Japanese word for "mission" (*shimei*) means to "use one's life." The important question, then, is, for whom and what purpose do we use our lives?

I have used my life to work whole-heartedly for the happiness of my fellow SGI members and the cause of world peace. My wish is that all of you will put your time to good use and grow into fine young people, and that each year you will feel proud that you did your very best. I also hope that someday you will come to use your precious time to contribute to the well-being of your parents and to the happiness and peace of people everywhere.

Procrastination Can Cause Suffering

All people have something they aren't good at and experience times when they just don't want to do what needs to be done. It may seem easier to put off the things we aren't good at or that we don't want to do. But the reality is that

the more we delay doing those things, the more they weigh on us and the more difficult they become to do. Putting off what we need to do only causes us to suffer later.

If you study and do your homework when you're supposed to, then you can use the rest of your time to do the things you enjoy. That is much more productive. Time to play and rest is also necessary. Use your days wisely, setting aside certain times to study, read, play, relax, and so on. When you make good use of your time in this way, you can add many more enjoyable and satisfying hours to your day.

I attribute my success to this: I never gave or took any excuse.

Florence Nightingale
1820–1910
Founder of Modern Nursing

How to
Deal With Your Mistakes

No Mistake Is Irredeemable

Nothing is irredeemable in youth. Rather, the worst mistake you can make when young is to give up and not challenge yourselves for fear of failure. The past is the past and the future is the future. Keep moving forward with a steady eye on the future, telling yourselves: "I'll start from today!" "I'll start fresh from now, from this moment!" This is the essence of Nichiren Buddhism, the Buddhism of true cause, the spirit to start from the present moment. This is the heart of chanting Nam-myoho-renge-kyo.

Mistakes Can = Progress

You mustn't view a mistake as a defeat. Especially for young people, mistakes and problems are actually a sign of progress. Because you're moving forward, there are bound to be headwinds. There are also times when you might stumble and fall. But when that happens, don't be discouraged. Just pick yourself up and set forth again.

The American animator and film producer Walt Disney (1901–66) said: "I think it's important to have a good hard failure when you're young. . . . I learned a lot out of that."[4]

Do not go around lamenting to others how hard it is for you to live in this world. To do so is an act utterly unbecoming to a worthy man.

—Nichiren

You Always Have a Second Chance

Happiness in life does not depend on how well things go in your youth. And no matter how many mistakes you make, you always have a second chance. Be ambitious and keep striving toward the future. If you don't do well in elementary school, try harder in junior high. If you don't do well in junior high school, do your best in high school. And if you're not happy with your achievements in high school, give it your all in university. If that's not to your satisfaction, there's still hope after graduation, as you challenge yourselves as active members of society. If you experience setbacks along the way, continue with a fighting spirit into your forties, fifties, sixties, and seventies.

All our dreams can come true, if we have the courage to pursue them.

Walt Disney
1901–66
Filmmaker, Animator, Founder of Disneyland

PHOTO: HULTON ARCHIVE/GETTY IMAGES

How to Avoid the Train Wreck of
Drugs & Alcohol

There's a Lot of Peer Pressure to Drink and Do Drugs. I Don't Want to Be Left Out. What Should I Do?

I can understand the feelings of young people when they sometimes want to take drugs or drink to be part of the group. But drinking alcohol or taking drugs in your teens is not an adventure that will contribute constructively to your life. And having free access to these things doesn't foster your freedom as a human being, as so many young people believe. If your friends drink and take drugs, look for a new group of friends.

Essentially, substance abuse can be pegged to one underlying condition—a lack of foresight and determination toward the future. So many youth have been robbed of the chance to fulfill their great potential because they did not maintain a focus on their goals. Pursuing fun in the moment led them to ruin. I believe you may be familiar with many famous examples, such as the superstar college basketball player who was drafted by the Boston Celtics. Expectations of him were so high, it seemed his presence would guarantee a championship team. Sadly, just before the beginning of his first season—before he even got a chance to play in his first pro game—he went to a party, overdosed on cocaine, and died. A tragic waste.

In so many ways, what separates those who go on to lead happy, fulfilling, and successful lives from those who do not are the choices they make during this crucial period. Those who choose to keep their dreams in sight weigh the importance of achieving

The truly cool are those who continue to make steady efforts to fulfill their dreams, even if their dedication goes unnoticed. (PHOTO: CLAUDIO CALDERON)

those dreams against the momentary "coolness" of surrendering to drinking and drugs and find such immediate gratification not worth the expense.

Master Your Mind

A Buddhist teaching urges, "Become the master of your mind rather than let your mind master you" (WND-1, 502). It encourages us to be the boss, exercising control over our minds, our thoughts, and our feelings—not to simply act on every impulse.

When you're under the influence of alcohol or drugs, it's like you're dancing in a dream. But when you wake from the dream, harsh reality awaits you. In addition, no matter how cool people who drink or take drugs may look, any strength or ability they show is not their own; it is the work of the alcohol or the drug.

In my opinion, the truly cool are those who continue to make steady efforts to fulfill their dreams, even if their dedication goes unnoticed and unrecognized by others. A person of self-control is free in the truest sense. It is therefore vital that you continue to challenge achieving your goals.

How to Recognize &
Develop True Courage

The Most Important Kind of Courage

We can find courage in many different areas of human endeavor. There is the courage to take part in an adventure and the courage that is needed to excel in sports, but this is only one aspect of courage. A more important kind of courage is that required to live a good life on a daily basis. For example, the courage to study hard or the courage to form and sustain good, solid friendships. This kind of courage we might even call perseverance, a virtue that sets our lives in a positive direction. This type of courage may not be showy, but it is really the most important.

What Is "True Courage"?

True courage—this is none other than having compassion for others. Mr. Toda thoroughly taught me this, and I've always put it into action.

From today, I would like all of you to remember that courage is ultimately compassion. Please uphold the jeweled sword of courage and compassion in your hearts. People lacking courage become cowardly and self-serving.

None of you who declare yourselves to be my disciples should ever give way to cowardice.

—Nichiren

What Does Courage Look Like in a Real, Daily Life Sort of Way?

Courage is the strength to live our lives the right way, to walk the right path. It can take many forms. For example, thinking what is the best way for your country and the world to achieve peace and then taking action to make that happen. That is the courage born of conviction.

Or thinking what you can do to contribute to people's happiness and make society better, and then working constructively toward that goal. That is the courage of love for humanity. Thinking as a mother what you can do for your children, or as a schoolteacher for your students, or how you can help and support your friends—this is the unpretentious courage of daily life.

SGI President Ikeda greets youth members, Tokyo, September 2002. (PHOTO: SEIKYO PRESS)

How to
Not Be Defeated by Illness

Illness Can Provide a Positive Opportunity

Health is a precious treasure. I spent my own youth battling illness. I suffered terribly from tuberculosis. I know, therefore, from personal experience how important good health is and what a blessing it is to have it.

There are undoubtedly young members who are struggling with illness right at this very moment. I say to you: please win in that struggle, living with invincible resolve and boldly fulfilling your great mission in this lifetime. I will continue praying with all my heart to banish the "devil of illness" from your lives.

Sickness can provide an opportunity for becoming stronger, for achieving a more profound state of life, and for encouraging others more meaningfully. It can be, quite literally, an opportunity for "changing poison into medicine."

That's why if you unexpectedly find yourself facing illness when you're young, it's important not to let it shock or depress you. Just keep a positive attitude, and face it with courage and optimism, saying to yourself: "I'm young. I can overcome this. This experience will allow me to achieve enormous growth as a person and to win in life."

Nam-myoho-renge-kyo is like the roar of a lion. What sickness can therefore be an obstacle?
—Nichiren

> Do not be afraid! Live out your lives boldly, as true lions!

Josei Toda
1900–58
Religious Revolutionist,
Second Soka Gakkai President

PHOTO: SEIKYO PRESS

The Struggle Against Illness Leads to Happiness

Having an illness doesn't necessarily mean that a person is unwell. That is not something that can be decided by other people or by society. True health is to be found in having a positive attitude toward life and a strong self that refuses to be defeated by anything.

A Serious Illness Can Shake a Person's Confidence and Spiritual Strength. How Can They Get It Back?

Falling ill is not a form of failure or defeat. It doesn't happen because our faith is weak. The hardship of illness that occurs when we are striving for kosen-rufu is simply the action of devilish influences trying to obstruct our attainment of Buddhahood. As such, we mustn't let illness intimidate us. Nichiren teaches us how to bring forth courage to face illness and attain Buddhahood in this lifetime. It is vital to rouse even stronger faith when you experience illness. Keep chanting Nam-myoho-renge-kyo with the determination to make this illness an opportunity to demonstrate the tremendous power of faith and achieve truly amazing growth as a human being.

How to
Deal With Money Issues

Is It Wrong to Want to Make Money? And How Can I Do So?

As long as we are living and working in society, having a certain amount of financial security is an important element for happiness. Josei Toda used to say, even though your wallet may be empty, there is an abundance of money floating about in the world—it just hasn't come your way, that's all!

> The consumption society has made us feel that happiness lies in having things, and has failed to teach us the happiness of not having things.

Elise Boulding
1920–2010
Sociologist, Peace Studies Pioneer

But, he would continue, if you accumulate good fortune, using it to drill a hole into that vast reservoir of money and tap some for yourself, you will never be in want.

Money Does ≠ Happiness

I know some of you may come from poor families and have difficulty paying your monthly school fees. Others among you may feel frustrated because you cannot buy the things you want. But you must realize that these are not uncommon situations. Many people have had similar experiences. Poverty is nothing to be ashamed of. What is disgraceful is to have an impoverished heart or to live dishonestly. Being born in a stately mansion is no guarantee of happiness, any more than being born in a shack dooms one to misery.

Many people today think that money equals happiness. They are making a grave mistake. Whether one is happy or unhappy depends not on how many material possessions one has. Even an affluent and seemingly enviable family can be struggling with some serious problem that may not be apparent. I once spoke with a world-renowned business-man who said: "Even though I have achieved fame and fortune, I felt a greater sense of purpose and fulfillment when I was poor. I had goals, and life was filled with chal-lenge." He went on, "I've recently come to understand that to regain that sense of fulfillment, I now have to contribute to the well-being and happiness of others."

His words are truly profound.

When you chant [Nam-myoho-renge-kyo], you should be aware that it is a more joyful thing than for one who was born blind to gain sight and see one's father and mother, and a rarer thing than for a man who has been seized by a powerful enemy to be released and reunited with his wife and children.

—Nichiren

How to
Improve Through Reading

Why Should I Read?

I'm sure there are all kinds of young people—some who like reading and some who don't. Even so, one thing is clear: Those who know the great joy of reading have richer lives, broader perspectives, than those who don't.

Encountering a great book is like encountering a great teacher. Reading is a privilege known only to human beings. No other living creature on this planet has the ability. Through reading, we come in contact with hundreds and thousands of lives, and commune with sages and philosophers from as long as two millennia ago.

The Right Way to Read

President Makiguchi said: "Don't read carelessly. You must ponder everything you read. It seems that many young people read but fail to think about the content. Thinking about what you read makes it part of you."

And President Toda offered more specific advice, saying: "There are many ways to read a book. One is to read only for pleasure, simply following the plot—this is a very shallow way to read. Another is to think about the author's motivation for writing the book, its historical backdrop, the societal elements of the time, the characters in the story, and the ideas and intention that the author is trying to express. And yet another way is to try to understand through the work what kind of person the author is or was, to grasp the writer's true character, ideals, beliefs, and views on life, the world, and the universe. If you don't take it this far, it cannot be called reading."

Those who know the great joy of reading have richer lives, broader perspectives, than those who don't. (PHOTO: EDWARD CHEN)

I Love Reading Comics. Is That OK?

If you read nothing but comics, of course it would hardly be beneficial! The most important thing is to develop yourselves. Some comic books do have positive messages that could change your life, open your eyes, or move you. Sometimes a comic book has a more profound message than a dull, monotonous book.

TV vs. Books

There is also the argument that comic books, along with television, stifle one's imagination. Both media provide the viewer with a prepackaged image. The strong point of literature, however, is that it lets you develop your imagination and ability to think.

There is a fundamental difference between the way you receive information from television and from books. Reading something in a book engraves it in your mind, in your life. It provides you with sustenance to grow. Just looking at something leaves you with only a surface impression—it's easy to do, and it gives you the illusion that by merely seeing something, you know all about it. This is only superficial understanding, though; it hasn't become a living, breathing part of you.

How to
Discover Your Mission & Dreams

How Do I Find Out What I'm Good At?

A saying goes that everyone has some kind of gift. Being talented doesn't mean just being a good musician, writer, or athlete—there are many kinds of talent. For instance, you may be a great conversationalist or make friends easily or put others at ease. Or you may have a gift for nursing, a knack for telling jokes, selling things, or economizing. You may be always punctual, patient, reliable, kind, or optimistic. Or you may love new challenges, be strongly committed to peace, or bring joy to others.

Each of us is as unique as a cherry, plum, peach, or damson blossom (see OTT, 200), as Nichiren Daishonin explains. Cherry blossoms and plum blossoms possess their own distinct wonder;

accordingly, you must bloom in the way that only you can.

Without a doubt, you each have your own jewel, your own innate talent within you. How can you discover that talent? The only way is to exert yourselves to the limit of your ability. Your true potential will emerge when you give everything you've got to your studies, sports, or whatever you take on.

What if I Don't Have Any Goals?

Do something, start something. As you make consistent efforts, you will begin to see your goals come into focus. You will discover your mission—the one only you can fulfill.

For example, it is important to develop skills in a field that you like or that interests you. The key is to have something you can take pride in, something you can challenge. It might be something like excelling in math, in a foreign language, in a sport, in an extracurricular activity, in making friends, or in doing volunteer work. The people around you may know you better in some areas than you do yourselves, so if you summon up the courage to ask them for advice, you might find the doors to new possibilities opening unexpectedly.

A person who has firm goals is way ahead of a person who has none. Setting goals is the starting point from which the construction of our life begins. Youth is a struggle to develop and shape oneself— an ongoing challenge to train oneself spiritually, intellectually, and physically.

What if I Don't Know Exactly What My Dreams Are or How to Achieve Them?

Your dream can be anything, even if it's vague right now. It can be a small thing. Don't think about whether it's something you can realize or not. The first step is to envision it. Once you've made up your mind, have the courage to

take the first step toward realizing it. Once you do so, the way forward will begin to reveal itself. Just keep pressing straight ahead. There will be times when you have doubts and second thoughts, and times when you hit a wall. All of these things are proof that you are growing. When you overcome the obstacle of your present limitations, new horizons will open up before you. That is why it's important to keep challenging yourself and keep persevering.

Mr. Toda said, "Young people should cherish dreams that seem almost too big to accomplish."

As teenagers, you are practicing Nichiren Buddhism, which teaches us how to achieve absolute victory in life. No prayer based on faith in the Mystic Law goes unanswered.

Prayer is the source of victory. When earnest prayer and arduous effort combine, dreams begin to come true.

How to
Turn Your Dreams Into Reality

You Are in Control of Your Destiny

You are the playwright of your own victory. You are also the play's hero. Shakespeare (1564–1616) wrote: "All the world's a stage, / And all the men and women merely players."

Buddhism teaches us that the individual writes and performs the script for his or her own life. Neither chance nor a divine being writes the script for us. We write it, and we are the actors who play it. This is an extremely positive philosophy, inherent in the teaching of "three thousand realms in a single moment of life."

You are the author and the hero. To perform your play well, it is important to pound the script into your head so thoroughly that you can see it vividly before your eyes.

Write Down Your Dreams— Then Chant!

Some of you may give up on doing something before even trying because you feel you wouldn't be good at it anyway. If you have this problem, I'd like to suggest a good way to challenge it.

Start by writing down your dreams or goals on a piece of paper. There's something really magical about the written word. Writing down what you want to do will put you on the path in that direction. By the way, scientists have also recently found that writing your goals down on paper stimulates the brain and makes you want to try to achieve those goals.

After writing down your goals, chant about them. Nichiren Daishonin says, "Nam-myoho-renge-kyo is like the roar of a lion" (WND-1, 412). Like the roar of a lion, the king of beasts, Nam-myoho-renge-kyo is the greatest source of strength that nothing can defeat. When you chant Nam-myoho-renge-kyo, the lion-like courage and determination to realize your goals and dreams will well up inside you. The next step is to take action.

Here, you might find it helpful to make a "Victory Notebook." It's not that difficult. Simply start by writing down all the things you want to do today and all the things you have to do today. Then decide on the order and time when you will do them. You can look at the notebook throughout the day to keep you on track and check off the items you complete. This is something you can do each day.

It's OK to Have Big Dreams

President Toda declared: "It's perfectly all right for youth to cherish dreams that may seem almost too big. What we can achieve in a single lifetime is always but a fraction of what we would like to achieve. So if you start out with expectations that are too low, you'll end up not accomplishing anything at all."

Of course, if you make no efforts, your dreams will amount to nothing but sheer fantasy. Effort and hard work construct the bridge that connects your dreams to reality. Those who make steady efforts are filled with hope. And hope, in turn, arises from steady efforts. Embrace your dreams and advance as far as they can carry you. That is the hallmark of youth.

Sometimes I Feel Like the Gap Between My Dreams and Reality Is So Huge That I Feel Powerless to Bridge It

That would seem to indicate that you have big dreams, and that in itself is wonderful. There's bound to be some kind of gap between our dreams and reality. Any dream that's easily attainable isn't very exciting. To realize our dreams, we need to have a strong commitment and determination to succeed.

Thomas Edison (1847–1931) was said to have been a poor student in school, but his strong desire to make life more convenient for everyone led him to become a great inventor. And for the Wright brothers (Orville 1871–1931; Wilbur 1867–1912), it was their enduring dream to be able to fly like a bird that enabled them to surmount a long series of failures and finally invent the first powered airplane. Though facing numerous obstacles and hardships, these great individuals continued to hold fast to their dream and worked tenaciously toward making it a reality. They never gave up on it, even when others said it was impossible or ridiculed them.

Dream Big, Be Committed to Kosen-rufu and All Your Dreams Will Be Realized

We embrace faith in the Mystic Law, which is the key to absolute victory. When we strive to achieve the great vow or wish for kosen-rufu based on this invincible faith, aiming for the peace and happiness of all humanity, our personal wishes and dreams will also definitely be realized. And even if things do not go exactly the way we hoped, we are nevertheless able to advance in the direction that is best for our individual lives. This is something in which we can have complete confidence when viewed from a long-term perspective.

PHOTO: CULTURE CLUB/GETTY IMAGES

Our greatest weakness lies in giving up. The most certain way to succeed is always to try just one more time.

Thomas Edison
1847–1931
Inventor of the Light Bulb and Phonograph

How to Chant So
That Awesome Things Happen

Is It Selfish to Chant to Be Taller or Better Looking?

Most prayers *are* selfish! You can chant for whatever you like. You can put your most cherished wishes and desires into your prayers, free of any pretense, in a way that is true to your own heart. Though you may not get results immediately, your chanting of Nam-myoho-renge-kyo will steadily move you in the right direction, and a horizon of boundless hope will open up for you without fail. You also have to make efforts, be resourceful, and take practical measures to make your prayers come true.

Be in Rhythm With the Universe

The universe and our lives are manifestations of the Mystic Law, Nam-myoho-renge-kyo. The Gohonzon is also an embodiment of Nam-myoho-renge-kyo. Since all are entities of the Mystic Law, they are essentially one and indivisible. Therefore, when we focus on the Gohonzon while chanting Nam-myoho-renge-kyo, our lives and the universe merge like cogs in a great machine meshing together with perfect precision, and we begin to move in the direction of happiness and fulfillment.

We can be in rhythm with the universe 365 days a year—in spring, summer, autumn, and winter—manifesting the vigor, wisdom, and good fortune with which to surmount any problem or suffering. When we rev up the powerful, revitalizing engine of Buddhahood, we can break through any impasse and boldly steer ourselves in the direction of hope and justice.

Is There a Specific Amount of Time I Should Chant?

Nichiren writes nothing about the specific amount we should chant. It is entirely up to each individual's awareness. Faith is a lifelong pursuit, so there's no need to be unnecessarily nervous or anxious about how much you chant, or to put unnecessary pressure on yourselves. Buddhism exists to free people, not to restrain them. Doing even a little bit every day is important. The food we eat each day turns to energy for our bodies. Our studies, too, become a valuable asset when we make steady efforts on a daily basis. Our lives are created from what we do, how we live, every day. For that reason, we should strive to live each day so as to continually improve ourselves. The driving force for this is our morning and evening practice.

Just be yourself when you chant. That's the most important thing. (PHOTO: ANTHONY WALLEN)

Is There a Right Way to Think or Pray When I'm Chanting?

Basically, just be yourself when you chant. That's the most important thing. Revere the Gohonzon as the fundamental basis of your life, reach out to it in your heart and take your problems to it—do this naturally, as a child reaches for its mother. When you're suffering or when you're sad, there's no need to put on a good face or pretend that everything's all right. Just chant exactly as you are, directly giving expression to the feelings in your heart.

Nichiren writes, "What is called faith is nothing unusual" (WND-1, 1036). And he urges, "Faith means putting one's trust in the Lotus Sutra . . . as parents refuse to abandon their children, or as a child refuses to leave its mother" (WND-1, 1036). In other words, all we need to do is trust the Gohonzon wholeheartedly, praying sincerely that our desires will be realized. Such prayer definitely will empower us.

There is nothing extraordinary about prayer—it is simply wishing for something with all our heart.

What's More Important: the Quality of or the Amount of Time I Spend Chanting?

The value—or, if you like, the quality—of a hundred dollar bill is more than a ten dollar bill. Naturally, most people would prefer a one hundred dollar bill, right? Similarly, in faith, sincere, strong prayers are important. Of course, having lots of one hundred dollar bills is even better! Likewise, in chanting Nam-myoho-renge-kyo to the Gohonzon, both quantity and quality count.

Everything you do in the realm of Buddhist faith and practice is for your own happiness. The main thing is that you feel deep satis-faction after chanting. There are no hard-and-fast rules about having to chant a certain number of hours. Setting chanting targets can be helpful, but when you're tired or sleepy and are just mumbling along in a half-conscious daze, it's better to stop and go to bed. After you've rested, you can chant with concen-tration and energy again. This is much more valuable. We should be alert and earnest when we pray, not nodding off.

As I said, most important is that our chanting be satisfying and refreshing, so that we can exclaim when we've finished, "Ah, that felt good!" By reinforcing that feeling day after day, our lives naturally move in the most positive direction.

I Chanted for Something and It Didn't Happen. Does That Mean Chanting Doesn't Work?

The Mystic Law's fundamental beneficial power is inconspicuous. When you pray for something, even though signs of your prayers being fulfilled may not be immediately apparent, the result will definitely appear in time. Underground water eventually comes to the surface. A seed that is planted waits until springtime to produce flowers. A certain time is required for a sapling to develop into a great tree.

By the same token, continuing Buddhist practice is very important. Buddhism is reason, after all. Even though people might have practiced faith with a fiery, almost fanatical fervor at one time, if they fail to continue, they cannot savor the true benefit of the Mystic Law.

On the other hand, even if, for instance, there are days when it is just not possible for you to do gongyo, you need not feel that you have been remiss in your practice. So long as you cherish the mind of faith, your good fortune will stay with you. Even chanting just one Nam-myoho-renge-kyo yields great benefit. The important thing is that you practice with strong and tenacious faith throughout your entire life.

I believe that those who continue to study throughout their entire lives can continually advance and realize victory in life. If you lose the spirit to advance and improve yourselves, you will stagnate, backslide, and ultimately experience failure in life.

How to Understand
Why Chanting Works

Buddhism Enables Us to Change Our Karma

The more we exert ourselves in faith, the greater the benefit we experience.

Of course, it's possible to get by in life without practicing Nichiren Buddhism. But sometimes we are confronted by karma over which we seem to have no control, or are buffeted about because of an inner weakness. What a tragic loss it would be if we could never change ourselves, if we could never exclaim confidently at the end of our days what a wonderful life we've led. That is precisely why a guiding philosophy in life is essential.

We Can Bring Out Our Best

By chanting Nam-myoho-renge-kyo, we can cleanse our lives of negativity and impurities. We can push everything in the direction of happiness. For example, a person's shyness can be transformed into valuable qualities such as prudence and discretion, while someone's impatience might be transformed into a knack for getting things done quickly and efficiently.

Just as poisonous compounds are changed into medicine, so these five characters of Myoho-renge-kyo change evil into good.
—Nichiren

Chanting Helps Us Transform Our Problems and Desires Into Happiness

Buddhism teaches the principle that "earthly desires are enlightenment." To explain this very simply, "earthly desires" refers to suffering and to the desires and cravings that cause suffering, while "enlightenment" refers to attaining a vast and expansive state of absolute happiness. Normally, one would assume that earthly desires and enlightenment are separate and distinct—especially since suffering would seem to be the exact opposite of happiness. But this is not the case in Nichiren Buddhism, which teaches that only by igniting the firewood of earthly desires can the flame of happiness be attained.

As a result, our lives are infused with the light and energy of happiness. Through chanting Nam-myoho-renge-kyo, we burn the firewood of our earthly desires.

When we chant Nam-myoho-renge-kyo, our problems and sufferings all turn into energy for our happiness, into fuel for our advancement.

The wonderful thing about faith in Nichiren Buddhism is its capacity to transform people's lives from the direst suffering into the greatest possible happiness and turn the most daunting problems into a source of growth and a foundation for human greatness.

Chanting Has a Far-Reaching Impact on Your Life

Our prayers have a far-reaching impact on our lives. Though you may chant to do well in your studies, the effect of your prayers will extend much further, rippling across the whole spectrum of your life.

When all is said and done, to want to sit in front of the Gohonzon and chant is very important. It is an expression of one's determination to improve oneself. That spirit is important. That spirit is proof of our humanity, an expression of our noble spirit to accomplish something with our lives.

Doing Gongyo Strengthens Our Life Force

Reciting the sutra is a daily activity in which we purify and prime our hearts and minds. In the morning, it is starting the engine for our day, like grooming ourselves before we set out for the day.

Some people have powerful engines, and some have weak engines. The strength of the engine dramatically affects what we accomplish throughout the course of our lives. The difference can be enormous.

Diligently applying ourselves in our daily practice of the sutra recitation boosts the power of our engine.

Reciting the sutra is a ceremony in which our lives commune with the universe. As we recite the sutra and chant Nam-myoho-renge-kyo, through our faith in the Gohonzon, we vigorously infuse the microcosm of our individual existence with the life force of the macrocosm, of the entire universe. If we do this regularly each morning and evening, our life force—or engine—is strengthened.

Chanting Recharges Our Inner Batteries

Chanting Nam-myoho-renge-kyo establishes a foundation of good fortune in young people's lives. If you establish a solid foundation now, there is no limit to the structure you can build upon it later. Many things contribute to building that foundation. Diligent application to one's studies helps, as does exercising to develop physical fitness and stamina.

But our inner state of life lies at the core of our mental and physical well-being. Buddhist practice is the only means by which we can strengthen, purify, and develop our inner life.

Chanting Nam-myoho-renge-kyo charges our batteries. If we take care to charge our batteries regularly, then we'll always be full of energy and vitality. If we fail to keep our batteries charged, we won't have energy when we need it most and as a result may be defeated by our environment.

Those who saturate their lives with Nam-myoho-renge-kyo and learn to keep their batteries charged while they're young are building a foundation for lifelong happiness.

How to Do Human Revolution to Create an Amazing Life & an Amazing World

What Is Human Revolution?

Human revolution is not something extraordinary or divorced from our daily lives. Here are some practical examples.

Let's say there's a young boy who spends all his time playing and never studies. Then, one day, he decides to try to improve his future chances, and he begins to take his studies seriously. That is his human revolution.

Or perhaps a woman seeks only happiness for her family on a superficial level. She's satisfied with her life until, one day, she asks herself: "What if our present happiness doesn't last? Maybe I should look for more solid, enduring happiness."

She begins practicing Nichiren Buddhism and, basing her life on this philosophy, starts working for her family's absolute happiness. That is her human revolution.

Or perhaps a father thinks only of his small world—himself, his family, and his friends. Then, one day, he decides to step out of these narrow confines just a little to extend a helping hand to the ill or suffering, giving earnest thought to how he can help them find happiness. As a result, he starts participating in SGI activities for that purpose. That is his human revolution.

In other words, human revolution is expanding your view beyond your restricted, ordinary, everyday world and striving for and dedicating yourself to achieving something more noble, more profound, more all-embracing.

The Most Fundamental of All Revolutions

There are all sorts of revolutions—political, economic, industrial, scientific, artistic, and those in distribution and communications. And there are many others. Each has its significance and, often, necessity.

But no matter what one changes, the world will never get any better as long as the people—the guiding force and impetus behind all endeavors—remain selfish and lack compassion. In that respect, human revolution is the most fundamental of all revolutions and, at the same time, the most necessary.

> I will seize fate by the throat; it shall certainly never wholly overcome me.

Ludwig van Beethoven
1770–1827
Composer

Examples of Human Revolution

When a seriously ill person recovers, that is great human revolution. When a mean person becomes kind, that is human revolution. When people who treat their parents poorly begin to respect and love them, that is human revolution.

Human revolution cannot be pinned down to one specific thing. It is any action that leads to positive change or improvement in the inner realm of our lives.

Human Revolution Seems Beyond Me. I Always Break My Resolutions as Soon as I Make Them

There's nothing wrong with that. If we were all perfect from the start, we wouldn't need to do human revolution!

In fact, those who at first may be completely overwhelmed by their environment or constantly defeated by their weaknesses but who then undergo a dramatic transformation as a result of solid Buddhist practice can be a wonderful inspiration for others.

The times we experience the most intense suffering, unbearable agony, and seemingly insurmountable deadlock are actually brilliant opportunities for us to carry out human revolution.

If you're the type whose resolve tends to melt away easily, if you find it difficult to stick to your goals, then just renew your determination each time you find yourself slipping. You will achieve your human revolution without fail if you keep struggling valiantly, pressing forward despite setbacks and disappointments, always thinking: "This time I'll make it! This time I will succeed!"

Can I Accomplish My Human Revolution Just by Reading Books on Philosophy or Ethics?

An uncountable number of such books have been written, as well as books on self-help and self-improvement. If human revolution could be achieved simply by reading, if we could change our destiny through the power of words alone, it would be an easy matter indeed.

The SGI is in pursuit not of abstract intellectual doctrine but of a thorough, real human transformation—in which people change their fundamental attitudes and ways of thinking and focus their minds, actions, and lives on the highest good. Essentially, this human revolution takes place when our lives are in the state of Buddhahood. When we fuse our lives with the enlightened life of Buddhahood, we can tap the power within to change ourselves fundamentally.

Become the Best Human Being Possible

A human being is a human being. No one can become anything more than human.

For that reason, the most important thing is simply to become the best human beings we can. No matter how we adorn ourselves with the trappings of fame, rank, academic credentials, knowledge, or wealth, if we are impoverished or bankrupt inside, our lives will be barren and empty.

What kind of people are we when all those externals have been stripped away? When we stand unadorned, except for our humanity? Human revolution is the challenge to change our lives at their core.

You Can Illuminate the World Around You

The great German poet and author Friedrich von Schiller (1759–1805) wrote: "As soon as it becomes light inside Man, there is also no longer any night outside him; as soon as it is calm within him, the storm in the universe is also lulled, and the contending forces of Nature find rest between abiding boundaries."[5]

The SGI represents a brilliant light of hope.

Everything begins from the human revolution of one person. It is important first and foremost that all of you win in life and in society. I also hope that with your brilliant presence, you will each illuminate all around you—the people you encounter, your local community, your country, and all of humanity.

Caption: SGI President Ikeda with members from Côte d'Ivoire during a monthly Soka Gakkai leaders meeting, Tokyo, March 2004. (PHOTO: SEIKYO PRESS)

YOU

&

OTHERS

Human relationships are like a mirror.

—Daisaku Ikeda

How to Understand
What True Friendship Is

Good Friends Encourage and Help One Another

You may think friendships just happen spontaneously and develop by themselves, but they must be infused with and supported by the eternally youthful spirit to grow and advance. They involve an unflagging commitment to always be there to encourage and help one another as you work toward your respective aims and goals in life. It is important to have some ambition—such as graduating from university or making a meaningful contribution to society. Friendships among people who lack a clear positive purpose or direction in life tend to be complacent and dependent in nature. Friendship among people who cheerfully encourage one another while striving to realize their dreams are the kind that deepen and endure.

What Is Friendship?

It is not simply a matter of being favorably disposed toward someone because he or she spends a lot of time with you, or lends you money, or is nice to you, or because you get along well and have a lot in common. True friendship implies a relationship where you empathize with your friends when they're suffering and encourage them not to lose heart, and where they, in turn, empathize with you when you're in the same boat and try to cheer you up. A friendship with those qualities flows as beautifully as a pure, fresh stream.

The purest and most beautiful stream that can be found in human existence is friendship. When the pure streams of friendship flowing from each person converge, they give rise to an even broader, deeper, and purer river of friendship, which will inspire all who see it to proclaim its beauty and clarity and want to drink from its waters.

There Are Different Kinds of Friendship, Aren't There?

I think we could call them the three levels of human relationships. In the first level of friendship, we see people forging bonds of mutual affection and empathy in the course of day-to-day activities. They seek to enjoy their lives together. It's friendship based on mutual enjoyment, on having a good time together.

The second level is a little more advanced. The friends have their own goals; they each have a clear vision of the kind of person they want to become, the kind of future they want to build, the kind of contribution they wish to make to humanity. So they encourage and support one another as they work to realize their dreams and make something of themselves in the world. This is a friendship of mutual encouragement.

The third level of friendship is the bond of comrades who share the same ideals, a friendship in which both would willingly give their lives for the other. This is the kind of friendship that exists in the realm of faith.

Many people who have achieved great things in history have had this kind of friendship.

But There Are Also Bad Friends, Who Can Exert a Negative Influence

Buddhism teaches that we should associate with good companions, meaning that we should be careful to choose good people as our friends and role models. It also instructs that we should distance ourselves from bad company. Nichiren, referring to a Buddhist scripture, states that even a good person who associates with evil people will, in two or three cases out of ten, be tainted by that evil (see WND-1, 310). We should therefore have the attitude, he says, to rebuke wrong, to rebuke destructive behavior.

By pointing out to someone that their actions are inflicting suffering and hurt on others, we can urge them to move in a more positive direction. Our honesty, in fact, can open the way to forging deep bonds of genuine friendship with that person. In other words, it's quite possible for a "bad" friend to become a good friend.

Our Friendships Can Determine the Direction of Our Lives

Nothing can compare to diamonds in brilliance and strength. How are diamonds polished? By other diamonds. In much the same way, people are polished by interacting with other people. When we connect with good people, our lives will begin to sparkle like diamonds, radiating the light of good. Meeting with good people helps us grow in a positive direction. On the other hand, if we listen to bad people, we will stop growing.

Nichiren Daishonin writes that if we mix with bad people, then we will naturally come to follow what they say perhaps two or three out of ten times, and will in the end become just like them (see WND-1, 310). I hope you never allow your pure lives to be muddied by such people.

The best way to attain Buddhahood is to encounter a good friend. How far can our own wisdom take us? If we have even enough wisdom to distinguish hot from cold, we should seek out a good friend.

—Nichiren

How to
Deal with Losing Friends

My Friend Doesn't Want to Talk to Me Anymore, and I'm Really Hurt

Young people's hearts are like sensitive thermometers. One minute you feel everything is great, and the next you suddenly feel so down you're convinced you must be the most worthless person in the world. You may also be overwhelmed by great sadness and despair because of problems with friends, heartache over love, or the illness of family members.

I assure you it is completely natural to experience such extremes of emotion and self-doubt while young, so you needn't compound your sadness by worrying that you feel that way. Rest assured that whatever your hardships, you will someday look back on them and they will all seem like a dream.

That said, it is important to recognize that as you go through such situations, the same is usually true for your friends. Therefore, the best thing to do is to have the courage to ask the friend who seems to be shunning you what's bothering her (or him). You will very likely find that the last thing she wanted to do was treat you coldly, and that in reality, while you neglected to find out what was wrong with her for fear of being hurt, she, too, was feeling rejected and lonely.

Human relationships are like a mirror. If you're thinking, "If only so-and-so were a little nicer to me, I could talk to him about how I feel," that person is probably thinking the same thing.

While it takes a bit of courage to make the initial attempt, a good plan would be to make the first move to open channels of communication. If, despite these efforts, you are still rebuffed, then the person you should feel sorry for is your friend.

We cannot read what's in another's heart; the human heart is much too complex. People change—it's as simple as that. If your friend shares the same feelings about the friendship as you do, then it is likely to last a long time. But if he or she decides to opt out, then it will be short-lived. You yourself may unintentionally let a friend down, causing a rift in your relationship. My advice is that you hold fast to your identity regardless of how others may appear to change.

If you are snubbed or let down by others, have the strength of character to vow that you will never do the same to anyone else. Though they usually do not realize it, those who betray others' trust are only hurting themselves. Those who intentionally hurt their friends are truly pathetic; it's as though they are driving a spike through their own hearts.

In any event, should a friendship end, there's no need to grow despondent. You don't have to beat yourself up, thinking every friendship must last forever. The important thing is that you remember the true meaning of friendship and that you make that true meaning the basis for your interactions with others.

How Do I Deal With Rejection?

Although it may seem difficult, if you are ignored, rejected, or made fun of, try not to be overly worried about it. According to Buddhist beliefs, those who treat others poorly make bad causes for which they unfortunately will experience the effects; they are truly to be pitied.

At the same time, remember that experiencing rejection and disappointment is an inevitable part of life. Nichiren, whose teachings we in the SGI follow, was also abandoned by many of his followers. I, too, have been betrayed by people whom I trusted and sincerely tried to encourage. But that is something I have learned is inevitable at times.

In the face of rejection, you must learn to be courageous. It is important to believe in yourself. Be like the sun, which shines on serenely even though not all the heavenly bodies reflect back its light and even though some of its brilliance seems to radiate only into empty space. While those who reject your friendship may sometimes fade out of your life, the more you shine your light, the more brilliant your life will become.

How to Have Amazing Friends...by
Being an Amazing Friend Yourself

A True Friend Always Has Your Back

Friendship depends upon you. It is your attitude that is important, not the other person's. Friendship is not simply a matter of the other person liking you and caring about your welfare. Nor is true friendship conditional, lasting only as long as the other person does not betray you or let you down. It is your concern and feelings for the other person that make a friendship. Friendship is never betraying a friend, even if he or she should betray you. Being friends with someone while they're experiencing good times but deserting them when they experience hard times cannot be called true friendship. Genuine friends have the courage to stick by a friend in even the worst situation, when everyone else has turned against him or her.

Chang-an writes, "If one befriends another person but lacks the mercy to correct him, one is in fact his enemy." The consequences of a grave offense are extremely difficult to erase. The most important thing is to continually strengthen our wish to benefit others.

—Nichiren

I Have Some Friends Who Engage in Dangerous Behavior, and I'm Worried About Them. How Can I Help Them?

The only way you can influence your peers is to establish genuine friendships with them one by one.

Listen attentively to what they have to say, but also clearly tell them when their ideas are wrong and admonish them not to ruin their lives through their actions. Develop the type of friendship in which you can say what needs to be said.

Nichiren teaches that if we befriend someone but lack the mercy to correct that person, we are in fact his or her enemy. How you convey your message to someone moving in the wrong direction is a matter of wisdom. Through serious contemplation based on your deep desire to help your friend, and through candid discussion with someone you trust—like a teacher or parent—you can find an upsurge of courage from within. This is what's behind the Buddhist chant of Nam-myoho-renge-kyo—it allows us to tap our inner wisdom and courage so that we can become the kind of people who truly care about and positively influence our friends.

As long as you genuinely care about others, your heart will definitely reach them some day. Even if someone breaks off with you for a while because of what you have said or done, the fact that you showed your sincerity will be etched in the depths of his or her life. The seed you plant in your friend's life will one day sprout in the form of a new and positive awareness that can propel that friend forward.

What Can I Say to a Friend Who Has Become Pregnant? Or to One Who's Been Lucky So Far but Is Having Sex and Not Being Careful?

Unwanted pregnancy is a tragedy. Young people have a tendency to feel invincible—that no matter what they do, things will be all right. But while this behavior is optimistic, in truth it is reckless. No one is free from the law of cause and effect.

For those who are sexually active but have been lucky so far, consider the following: To have an abortion, especially while very young, can be spiritually depressing and physically risky. And if you decide to go through with an unexpected pregnancy, you will more than likely have to sacrifice your freedom to enjoy activities in which others can freely participate. Your teen years are a period to build the foundation of your future happiness. It is the age when your body and mind are still very fresh and flexible, and you can absorb many things that will be important to you for the rest of your life. It is the age when you can master some skills or devote

yourself to studying, in which you can freely shape your future as you please. It would be tragic to give up such great freedom so young. You will be doing a disservice not only to yourself but to your parents and others who have been caring so much about you over the years.

For your friend who became pregnant, I believe it is vital that you maintain a genuine friendship with her. That doesn't mean merely sympathizing with her but providing her with the strength to stand up for herself. Your friend may be hurting or at a loss. While respecting her decisions, I hope you can continue to encourage her. Tell her that no matter how difficult her immediate circumstances, she can absolutely turn her situation into something joyful. Of course, this should not be a rationale for throwing caution to the wind. It's just that no matter where we find ourselves, we should always maintain hope.

How to
Deal with Frenemies

How Can I Transform a Negative Situation With a Former Friend Into a Positive One?

Through the power of our deep and strong resolve, chanting Nam-myoho-renge-kyo is the ultimate means for bringing harmony to people in our environment and transforming them into a positive force for value creation. In addition, praying for others' happiness and welfare is the action of a Buddha. There is no higher or nobler state of life.

Mr. Toda often used to say: "The Lotus Sutra states: 'Although the devil and the devil's people will be there, they will all protect the Buddhist Law'. If you have strong faith, you can transform anyone into an ally who will support the noble cause of human happiness and unsurpassed good that is kosen-rufu. It's amazing how this works. That's why nothing is better than chanting!"

Through chanting Nam-myoho-renge-kyo, we can transform any relationship into a fortunate Buddhist connection, any person into a positive "good friend."

What Should I Do if Someone Speaks Ill of Me Behind My Back?

Never be afraid of that. Just brush it off. Even the world's greatest people were criticized and belittled.

How to Help Your Friends When
They Are Suffering

What's the Best Way to Help Other People?

What's crucial is the sincere wish to see others become happy. And it is something we should make some effort toward each day. Mr. Makiguchi often talked about classifying goodness into acts of small, medium, and great consideration.

For example, imagine you have a friend who constantly needs money. Giving your friend money is an act of small good, whereas helping your friend find a job is an act of medium good.

If your friend is suffering because of a tendency to be irresponsible and lazy, however, then neither a gift of money nor a job will help. The money will be squandered, and your friend will doubtless lose the job through his or her negative habits. Great good means helping that person face and uproot the lazy nature that is the source of your friend's suffering—in other words, demonstrating and helping to teach a correct belief system.

How Do I Become a Person Who Can Really Touch People's Lives?

A person's nobility is manifested in compassion for others. Kindness and consideration for others resonate with both the Buddhist concept of compassion and the core Christian concept of love. When viewed from a larger perspective, we exist here thanks to the warmth, kindness, and support not only of the people around us but of everything on this earth and in the entire universe.

All living things—flowers, birds, the sun, the soil—support one another in a beautiful symphony of life. Since the birth of this planet more than four billion years ago, life form after life form have been conceived and nourished. Human life is a part of that chain. If at any point a link were missing from this chain, none of us would be alive today. We are all proof that the chain hasn't been broken.

Life produces new life—surely this is consideration in its most basic form. Delving deeper into this idea, I think we can say that the earth itself is a giant living organism filled with consideration. The activity of the entire universe is essentially a function of compassion.

Truly commendable people have the spirit to improve and grow, and continually striving to develop ourselves above all else is true consideration for others.

A good believer is one who does not depend upon persons of eminence or despise those of humble station; who does not rely on the backing of superiors or look down on inferiors; who, not relying upon the opinions of others, upholds the Lotus Sutra among all the sutras. Such a person the Buddha has called the best of all people.

—Nichiren

How Gratitude Makes You
More Human

Be Truly Beautiful

People whose hearts are full of gratitude and appreciation are truly beautiful. A humble heart is the wellspring of great growth and development.

Be Mature

To feel gratitude to one's parents sounds like a trivial thing, but this is the mark of true maturity and growth as a human being.

Elevate Your Lives

The ungrateful feel that it is below them to show any kind of appreciation. They are under the delusion that showing gratitude to others diminishes their own worth. But it is this sense of appreciation that elevates, enriches, and expands the human spirit. A lack of gratitude is actually a sign of arrogance.

The Proper Way for a Human to Live

None of us can exist in isolation. Our lives and existence are supported by others in seen and unseen ways, be it by parents, mentors, or society at large. To be aware of these connections, to feel appreciation for them, and to strive to give something back to society in a spirit of gratitude is the proper way for human beings to live.

> If the only prayer you say throughout your life is "Thank you," then that will be enough.

Elie Wiesel
1928–
Author, Holocaust Survivor, Nobel Peace Prize Winner

How to Tell If You're in a
Healthy Romantic Relationship

What Is the Difference Between a Healthy Relationship and an Unhealthy One?

The true purpose of your studies and participation in club or team activities is to build a foundation for a strong self. Your problems too—be they a lack of self-confidence or a strained relationship with a friend—enable you to construct a solid core.

The same can be said about love. It should be a force that helps you expand your lives and bring forth your innate potential with fresh and dynamic vitality. That is the ideal, but, as the saying "love is blind" illustrates, people often lose all objectivity when they fall in love.

The question is: Does the person you like inspire you to work harder at your studies or distract you from them? Does her presence make you more determined to devote

greater energies to school activities, be a better friend, a more thoughtful son or daughter? Does he inspire you to realize your future goals and work to achieve them? Or is that person your central focus, overshadowing all else—your school activities, your friends and family, and even your goals?

If you are neglecting the things you should be doing, forgetting your purpose in life because of the relationship you're in, then you're on the wrong path. A healthy relationship is one in which two people encourage each other to reach their respective goals while sharing each other's hopes and dreams. A relationship should be a source of inspiration, invigoration, and hope.

Being in Love Feels Amazing. Sometimes I Don't Want to Focus on School; I Would Rather Focus on My Boyfriend

Please don't succumb to the view that love is the be-all and end-all, deluding yourselves that, as long as you are in love, nothing else matters. Nor, I hope, will you buy into the misguided notion that sinking ever deeper into a painful relationship is somehow romantic.

All too often, when a relationship ends, the great passion it once inspired seems nothing more than an illusion. The things you learn through studying, on the other hand, are much more permanent. It is important, therefore, that you never extinguish the flame of your intellectual curiosity.

Please don't live without direction but, rather, pursue lives of meaning and purpose. Just as a house will be uninhabitable if its foundations are laid carelessly, it's clear what kind of results you can expect if you take shortcuts or neglect to make proper efforts. In that respect, it is certainly not wise to try to act like adults before you can properly look after yourselves.

The important thing is for you to do your very best in the endeavors you have to concentrate on now. Through such efforts, you will grow into individuals who have truly wonderful futures ahead of you. I hope you will not sell yourselves short and stifle your vast and limitless potential before it even has a chance to bloom. Far too many people nip their brilliant promise in the bud because of their blind pursuit of love.

How to End Up in
a Great Relationship

Don't Get Stuck Being Lovestruck

Rather than becoming so lovestruck that you create a world where only the two of you exist, it is much healthier to learn from those aspects of your partner that you respect and admire and continue to make efforts to improve and develop yourself. Antoine de Saint-Exupéry (1900–44), the author of *The Little Prince*, once wrote, "Love is not two people gazing at each other, but two people looking ahead together in the same direction."[6] It follows then that relationships last longer when both partners share similar values and beliefs.

Strong Self-Identity Leads to Real Love

Real love is not two people clinging to each other; it can only be fostered between two strong people secure in their individuality. A shallow person will have only shallow relationships. If you want to experience real love, it is important to first sincerely develop a strong self-identity.

If one gives food to others, one will improve one's own lot, just as, for example, if one lights a fire for others, one will brighten one's own way.

—Nichiren

How to Avoid Ending Up in
a Bad Relationship

Some Young Women Find Themselves in Relationships Where They Get Hurt Emotionally, or Even Physically. How Do I Avoid This?

Some young women prove extremely vulnerable to the insistent advances of the opposite sex. They act as though stunned and lose their ability to make calm, rational decisions. It is precisely for this reason that young women must develop inner strength and self-respect. Since they are the ones who most often get hurt, they have every right to assert their dignity and look after their welfare. And if the young man in question does not respect this right, then he isn't worth being with.

With some people, however, once they have gotten into a relationship, they have a hard time saying no to the other person for fear it will be taken as a lack of commitment. In such cases, love becomes like riding in a car with no brakes. Sometimes, even if you want to get out, you cannot; even if you regret having gotten in, the car won't stop. People often get involved in relationships thinking they are free and independent but at some point find they have become captive to the relationship.

Each of you is infinitely precious. Therefore, I hope you will treat yourselves with utmost respect. Please do not follow a path that will cause you suffering; rather, take the road that is best for your well-being.

The truth is, ideal love is fostered only between two sincere, mature, and independent people. It is essential, therefore, that each of you work on polishing yourself first.

How Can I Tell if I'm in a Bad Relationship?

If the relationship you're in is causing your parents to worry or making you neglect your studies or engage in destructive behavior, then you and the person you're seeing are only being a negative influence and hindrance to each other. Neither of you will be happy if you both end up hurting each other.

No matter how much you may appear to be enjoying yourselves now, or how serious you think you are about your relationship, if you allow your love life to consume all your time and energy to the detriment of your growth, then you're just playing a game. And if you're always playing games, then your life will be just that, a game.

Regardless of how large a number is, if multiplied by zero, it will inevitably come to zero. To have a relationship that wipes out the value in your life is truly sad.

Be Wise and Don't Get Used

The fact is, some boys are only out to use girls to satisfy their sexual impulses. So girls have to be on their guard and cultivate their powers of wisdom and judgment in order to see through such people. Girls, too, can initiate sexual relationships, though usually their motivation is to deepen the relationship, which can easily backfire.

Worthy persons deserve to be called so because they are not carried away by the eight winds: prosperity, decline, disgrace, honor, praise, censure, suffering, and pleasure.

—Nichiren

My Boyfriend Wants to Have Sex With Me. I Love Him and Don't Want to Lose Him. What Should I Do?

That young people are interested in many things, including sex, is a natural part of their growth as human beings. You may have life-long regrets, however, if you are blindly carried away by your physical desires.

The urge to explore that aspect is very strong, fueled by both your body and your mind, so it is important to have the right attitude and understand that the decisions you make today, the actions you take, have consequences. Your future does not exist in some far-off place. The seed for your future happiness lies in your behavior today, your frame of mind at this very moment. Therefore, it is important to think about the best kind of relationship you can have with friends, sweethearts, and anyone important to you. If you fall in love, I hope you will remember that, ultimately, the best relationship is one in which both you and your partner can continue to develop yourselves.

The tendency for teens, especially, is to be blind in love. But I have to tell you, love means more than just doing whatever your boyfriend suggests. It concerns me that too many teenagers become pregnant or contract illnesses and suffer for a long time, sometimes permanently, as a result of momentary passions.

The ideal relationship is one in which you mutually aim at a great future goal, encouraging and helping each other develop. If your boyfriend really cares about you, he will not force you to do anything you don't want to do. By saying no firmly, you can see just how genuine his sincerity is.

I hope you will take the course of action that supports the sort of future you dream of and that you are not swayed by others' notions of what is cool.

How to
Deal with Heartbreak

I Fall Into Deep Despair and Feel Like I Can't Go On After a Bad Breakup. How Can I Change This?

Many people can probably relate to such feelings. But you are only letting yourselves down if you succumb to unhealthy obsessions in your youth or are so blinded by love that you cannot see anything else. No matter what, you must always do your best to live courageously. You mustn't be weak-hearted. Youth is a time for advancing bravely into the future. You must not veer off course, fall behind, or hide in the shadows.

Youth is not a time for pessimism, self-pity, or sadness. Such a mind-set is for losers. Please have the confidence and fortitude to think to yourselves when you face rejection, "It's their loss if they cannot appreciate how wonderful I am!" This is the kind of resilient spirit you must strive to cultivate.

I'm sure quite a few among you have had your hearts broken or been badly hurt and perhaps felt unable to go on, your self-esteem in tatters. But you must never believe that you are worthless. There is no substitute for you, who are more precious than all the treasures in the universe. No matter what your present circumstances, I think of all of you as my irreplaceable sons and daughters, and I have the greatest expectation that you will overcome all obstacles and rise out of any suffering and despair.

How Should I View My Heartbreak From a Buddhist Perspective?

Only when we experience the crushing, painful depths of suffering can we begin to understand the true meaning of life. Precisely because we have experienced great suffering, it is imperative that we go on living.

The important thing is to keep moving forward. If each of you uses your sadness as a source of growth, you will become a person of greater depth and breadth— an even more wonderful you. This is the harvest of your pain and suffering.

Hold your head high. Because you have lived with all your might, you are victors. You must not sink into depression or take a path that leads to self-destruction.

Though one might point at the earth and miss it, though one might bind up the sky, though the tides might cease to ebb and flow and the sun rise in the west, it could never come about that the prayers of the practitioner of the Lotus Sutra would go unanswered.

—Nichiren

How to Deal with
Getting Into a College

What if I Can't Get Into the College That's My Top Choice?

Not attending the school of your choice may certainly be disappointing. But viewed in the long term and from the essential point of study, it doesn't really matter that you graduate from a well-known school.

I studied at night school. Like many others in those turbulent years following World War II, I had no money, so I had to work during the day to put myself through school in the evening. It was a painful struggle, but an experience of which I will always be proud.

Later, President Toda tutored me privately. He taught me everything he had learned. He once told me, "Become an inspiration for those who cannot attend good schools." Those who start out under difficult circumstances and go on to become first-rate individuals can be sources of hope and inspiration for many. Please remember always that academic background isn't everything.

At any rate, since you have been accepted to a school—even if it is not your first choice and regardless of how society judges it—it's important to decide that the place where you are is the very best, that it is the perfect place for you to learn all you want. This way of thinking is far more constructive and beneficial in the long run.

I Didn't Get Into a Prestigious College. Will This Affect My Success in the Future?

The school you graduate from doesn't determine your entire life. Far more important is that you have the strength and depth of character

to earnestly ponder the question "How should I live my life?" How much inner strength and depth you possess will determine how satisfying your life will be.

Your future is not determined by the school you graduate from. It's determined by you and who you are as a human being.

I'm Not Sure Whether I Should Attend a Vocational School, a Two-Year College, or a Four-Year University. What Is Best for My Future?

In today's society, the person with a specialty in a given vocational field may have an advantage in finding work. But I also think it is an important and wonderful thing for students to attend a four-year college, as many of their parents may wish, and pursue a more specialized field later. Attending a university and exposing yourself to a wide range of learning is a good way to refine and cultivate your intellect and develop yourself overall. Higher education is an important tool for building character too.

Extensive learning is something common to people of refinement and culture the world over. Such education provides the opportunity to rise to a high level of personal development.

Education can be likened to climbing a mountain. The higher you climb, the broader your field of vision becomes and the wider the world that unfolds before you. You begin to see things that you could not see before. The question of where to study—whether at a vocational school, a two-year college, or a four-year university— is something that only you can decide based on many factors, including your family circumstances, academic ability, and personal goals and ambitions. If you make the decision yourself, you'll have no regrets later. Of course, in deciding what to do, it is important to consult others— your parents, teachers, seniors, and friends. But once you make your decision and put it into action, don't look back. You mustn't live a life filled with indecision and lingering regret.

The Purpose of Education Is to Serve Others

The proud mission of those who have received an education must be to serve, in seen and unseen ways, the lives of those who have not had this opportunity. At times, education may become a matter of titles and degrees and the status and authority these confer. I am convinced, however, that education should be a vehicle to develop in one's character the noble spirit to embrace and augment the lives of others.

Education should provide in this way the momentum to win over one's own weaknesses, to thrive in the midst of society's sometimes stringent realities, and to generate new victories for the human future.

PHOTO: GIANLUIGI GUERCIA/AFP/GETTY IMAGES

It's the little things citizens do. That's what will make the difference. My little thing is planting trees.

Wangari Maathai
1940–2011
Nobel Peace Prize Winner, Environmentalist, "Tree Lady"

How to
Get the Most out of School

Why Is Studying Even Important?

Top athletes not only train their bodies, but many of them also study about how the body works and about nutrition and other related fields. I know many actors and entertainers who read a huge number of books to polish their performance abilities and help them play their roles.

I hope you'll look at your present school studies as laying the foundation for being able to freely study whatever you like in the future. You'd be amazed at how things that don't seem relevant at the time turn out to be incredibly useful later in life. Just try to make a start in some area. Begin by making a small effort.

Being good or bad at studying is really just a matter of whether or not you apply yourself.

You may find your studies now very boring, but in the process of studying you will break out of the shell of your small self into the freedom of a much broader, greater realm. Your life will be illuminated. Learning is light.

Those who press on with their studies with a positive attitude, no matter what, are the ones who win out in the end.

How Does Studying Have Any Relevance to My Future?

When a building is being constructed, the foundation doesn't really give us any idea of what the finished structure will look like. At the same time, when the building is completed, the foundation is no longer visible. Even so, it is that foundation that keeps the building standing for decades or even centuries.

The same is true of study. Each effort to challenge yourself contributes to building your foundation.

I'm Discouraged About My Grades. What Should I Do?

Grades are not a true measure of your worth as a person. Don't compare yourself to others, and don't allow your grades to make you lose your self-confidence.

Instead, you can make improving your grades a goal to strive for. You can try to raise them a little at a time. I hope you will challenge yourselves in your studies in this way.

Even if you don't achieve the results you'd hoped for, the efforts you are making are undoubtedly contributing to your growth and development.

Over the long term, your grades are much less important than acquiring the habit of learning and self-improvement. A person who is always ready and eager to learn creates a life of infinite possibility.

It is never too late to begin studying in earnest. As long as you don't give up on yourself, you can have the lowest grades in the class and still get better—and when you do, it will mean even more to you, because of where you started. The worst thing is to let a failure to improve your grades make you stop studying.

Success is a matter of perseverance. It's important to make a real effort, to try your hardest. You can't expect results in a day. Keeping at it is what matters.

Misfortune will change into fortune. Muster your faith, and pray to this Gohonzon. Then what is there that cannot be achieved?

—Nichiren

How to
Think About a Career

I Wonder If I Have What It Takes to Get the Job I Want

Life is long. The real result of your daily efforts will be revealed in your forties, fifties, and sixties. So it is important that each of you find something—it doesn't matter what—with which to challenge yourself while young. Regard youth as the time to study and train yourself.

We each have a unique mission that only we can fulfill. But that doesn't mean you should simply wait for someone to tell you what yours is, doing nothing until then. It is fundamental that you discover your mission on your own.

Precious gems start out buried underground. If no one mines them, they'll stay buried. And if they aren't polished once they've been dug out, they will remain in the rough.

People should constantly strive to unearth the jewel in their lives and polish it. There are countless examples of people who did not stand out in high school but who struck a rich deposit of hidden potential when they entered society and gained life experience. Therefore, getting a job is just the starting point in uncovering your true ability; it is absolutely not the final goal. There is no need to be impatient. It is important that you make your way up the mountain of life steadily, without rushing or giving up.

> Satisfaction of one's curiosity is one of the greatest sources of happiness in life.

Linus Pauling
1901–94
Chemist, Nobel Peace Prize Winner

I Have No Idea What I Want to Do in the Future

Why not start out with a job you can get easily, something you are familiar with? That way you can gain practical experience and find out what you're good at.

Many young people may be under the impression that it is better to work for a large corporation or a government agency than for a small, unexciting business. But often this is not the case. There are so many things you just won't understand until you actually start working. Plus, there are as many kinds of companies as there are people.

Therefore, it is important to have the inner strength and common sense to learn everything you can where you are, to develop the means by which to support yourselves, to pursue substance rather than the ephemeral, and to explore the depths of your potential. It is vital that you become irreplaceable wherever you are.

You have the right to decide what type of job you want to do; the choices are open. Having said that,

however, many jobs do require a certain level of academic qualification and experience.

Some people start working right out of high school, either by choice or because of their family situation. Others join the work force after graduating from college, while others become homemakers. Some people aim to become public servants, and still others strive to gain technical proficiency in some field. The bottom line is that there are many different options, all of which you are at liberty to choose from.

What Should I Look for in a Job?

Mr. Makiguchi taught that there are three kinds of value: beauty, benefit, and good. In the working world, the value of beauty means to find a job you like; the value of benefit is to get a job that earns you a salary that can support your daily life; the value of good means to find a job that helps others and contributes to society.

But not many can find the perfect job from the start. Some may have a job they like, but it isn't putting food on the table; or their job pays well, but they hate it. That's the way things go sometimes. Also, some discover that they're just not cut out for the career they dreamed of and aspired to.

President Toda said that the most important thing is to first become indispensable wherever you are. Instead of moaning that a job differs from what you'd like to be doing, he said, become a first-class individual at that job. This will open the path leading to your next phase in life, during which you should also continue doing your best. Such continuous efforts are guaranteed to land you a job that you like, that supports your life, and that allows you to contribute to society.

What if I Set Out to Achieve One Thing and Then Change My Mind?

That's perfectly all right. Few people started out with the ambition of doing what they're doing.

My experience was that I wanted to be a newspaper reporter, but my poor health prevented me. Today, however, I have become a writer who can hold his own in the literary world.

The important thing is to develop yourselves in your present situations, to take control of your growth.

Once you have decided on a job, I hope you will not be the kind of people who quit at the drop of a hat and are always insecure and complaining. Nevertheless, if after you've given it your all you decide that your job isn't right for you and you move on, that's perfectly all right too. My concern is that you don't forget you are responsible for your environment when you make your decision.

Taking your place as a member of society is a challenge; it is a struggle to survive. But wherever you are is exactly where you need to be, so you must strive there to the best of your ability.

A tree doesn't grow strong and tall within one or two days. In the same way, successful people didn't get to where they are in only one or two years. This applies to everything.

I Want to Work for World Peace

Aspiring to devote oneself to a humanistic cause, to upholding human rights and spreading the ideals of Buddhism out of a desire to work for the people's happiness and welfare, is a truly laudable ambition.

That does not mean, however, that you cannot contribute to peace unless you are in some special profession. Of course, while I highly commend anyone who wishes to work for the United Nations or become a volunteer worker overseas, there are many people striving for peace in their own, humble specialties.

The main thing is to be proud of your work and your capacity, to live true to yourselves. Many revolutionaries throughout history have lost their lives in the struggle for reformation. Theirs, too, was a worthy vocation.

At any rate, I want each of you to be active in all fields. Activity is another name for happiness. What's important is that you give free, unfettered play to your unique talents, that each of you live with the full radiance of your being. This is what it means to be truly alive.

If in this present existence I am so fearful for my life that I fail to speak out, then in what future existence will I ever attain Buddhahood? Or in what future existence will I ever be able to bring salvation to my parents and my teacher? With thoughts such as these uppermost in my mind, I decided that I must begin to speak out.

—Nichiren

How to Deal with
Parent & Family Issues

How Can I Be Happy When My Parents Are So Messed Up? Sometimes I Wish I Had Better Parents

Every family has its own set of circumstances and problems that only its members can fully understand. You may wonder why you were born into your family. Or why your parents aren't as kind as others. Or why you are not blessed with a more beautiful home and a more loving and supportive family. You may even want to leave home. One thing I can say, however, is that no matter what kind of people your parents are, they are *your* parents. If you did not have them, you would not be alive. Please understand the deep significance of this point. You were born to this particular family in this particular place and on this planet Earth at this particular time. You were not born into any other family. This fact encompasses the meaning of everything.

Buddhism explains that nothing happens by chance and that people already possess within them all that they need to be happy. Therefore, there is no treasure more precious than life itself. No matter how difficult your situation, no matter how much you feel ignored by your parents, you are alive now—still young and blessed with a youthful spirit with which you can construct the happiest of lives from this moment forward. Do not destroy or harm your precious future by giving way to despair today.

Courageously spur yourself on, reminding yourself that the deeper the pain and grief, the greater the happiness that awaits you. Have the determination to become a pillar of support for your family.

Buddhism teaches this way of life. Whether you have a parent suffering from alcoholism or a serious illness, whether your family is experiencing difficult times because of a parent's failed business, whether you have to endure the pain of seeing a parent criticized and attacked even falsely, or whether you are abandoned by a parent—all of these seemingly adverse situations can be viewed as nourishment to make you grow even stronger.

Regardless of how you are treated by your parents, ultimately, it is your responsibility, not theirs, that you become happy. It is up to each of us to have the determination to become the "sun" that can dispel all the darkness in our lives and within our families. Nichiren Buddhists know that this resolve can be fortified by chanting Nam-myoho-renge-kyo each morning and evening.

You Can Transform Your Family

There are many people, many lives, on this planet, too numerous, in fact, to count. From this great multitude, we wondrously find ourselves together with those in our families— as parents and children, as brothers and sisters, as husbands and wives. If we do not live joyfully and cheerfully in the company of those with whom we share this profound bond, what is life for? Should the atmosphere at home be somber, you yourself can be the "sun." By being a shining presence, you can cast the light of hope on your father, mother, and whole family. It is not the environment—it is you. If you are strong, you can absolutely bring about a transformation in your family and your surroundings.

My Parents Are Always Nagging Me. I Can't Stand to Be Home for More Than Ten Minutes!

How often have I heard that! While, of course, there are those who have good, open family communication, many young people get angry at their parents for telling them what to do. Often they end up not speaking to them at all.

I, too, fought with my mother from time to time about how I chose to live my life. I'd say: "Leave me alone! Let me do things my way!"

Mothers and fathers always seem to be giving their kids a hard time. From prehistoric times, mothers have been saying things like: "Do your homework!" "Turn off the television!" "Wake up or you'll be late!" It's not something we can change. But you'll understand how your parents feel when you become a parent yourself.

So it is important for you to be big-hearted. If a parent yells at you, you can think: "A loud voice means she is healthy; that's great," or, "Oh, he is expressing his love for me. I appreciate it." Your ability to view parents in this way is a sign of your increasing maturity.

Throughout the animal world, parents teach their young how to survive—how to hunt, how to eat, etc. Accordingly, our parents teach us so many things, launching us in the right direction. This is some-thing we learn to appreciate as we become adults ourselves.

I think it's important that you use your own wisdom to avoid fighting with your parents. Furthermore, when your parents quarrel between themselves, as many do from time to time, the wisest thing is for you to stay out of it.

What if I'm the Only Person in My Family That Practices Nichiren Buddhism?

An Argentine proverb says, "The sun rises for everyone." If one person in a family decides to practice Nichiren Buddhism, it is as if the sun has risen to shine on his or her entire family. Through the beneficial power of faith in the Mystic Law, you will be able to lead your whole family in the direction of happiness and enlightenment. There's no need to be anxious or impatient. The power of the Mystic Law is absolute. In the end, everyone in your family will be embraced by that power.

Some Kids Are Sad Because They Don't Have a Mom or Dad

I know how those of you who are in this situation must feel. But you are all young lions. I hope you will be strong, positive, and self-confident. If you don't have a father, then be twice as good to your mother, and likewise, if you don't have a mother, be doubly supportive of your father.

For those of you who have experienced the death of a parent, please know that they remain alive in your heart. When you chant to the Gohonzon, they are also embodied therein. You are connected together through your chanting. Your deceased mother or father is always watching over your growth. They are applauding your efforts, without a doubt.

In a letter to a follower whose mother had passed away [the father having also died sometime earlier], the Daishonin writes to the effect: "Your head is the head of your parents, your feet are their feet, your ten fingers are their ten fingers, your mouth is their mouth" (see WND-2, 658).

This means that all the benefit you gain through your efforts for kosen-rufu, using the body that you received from your parents, will flow on to the lives of your parents as well.

When you are victorious, your parents are victorious.

Soka University of America campus, Aliso Viejo, California. (PHOTO: SOKA UNIVERSITY OF AMERICA)

How & Why to Show
Appreciation to Your Parents

No Matter How Hard I Try, I Can't Respect My Parents

That's all right for now. Remember, you are who you are, aside from your parents. Just strive to become the best person you can. This is your precious youth.

If you have tough problems at home that you can't deal with on your own, please find a trusted senior in faith you can talk to. But don't forget that you owe your parents a great debt of gratitude simply for giving you the gift of life. Parents are people too. They aren't perfect. I hope you will try to be mature enough to imagine their problems and the things they are going through.

Aware that some young people had difficulties with their parents, Mr. Toda still made the strict point that those who are unable to have compassion for their parents would not be able to carry out kosen-rufu. The bonds of parent and child are mysterious and have unfathomably deep meaning. Viewed from the profound perspective of Buddhism, we have chosen to be born to our parents so that we may fulfill our great mission in this lifetime. Therefore, having appreciation for our parents is an expression of gratitude for being born and being alive. The wish to repay this debt of gratitude that we owe our parents enables us to open up and expand our life condition.

Also, please remember that your fellow members of the Soka family are always there, ready to share your problems and sufferings and to chant together with you. I am also with you.

Let's cheerfully usher in a new year of bright promise, with our hearts open and filled with joy!

Try to Understand Where Your Parents Are Coming From

Even parents who are extremely critical, or who are attached to outdated ways of thinking and have little understanding of the younger generation, can be motivated by an intense concern for their children and be willing to undergo any sacrifice for their children's welfare. When children go the extra mile to try to understand their parents' hearts, they can make dramatic strides in deepening their own character and developing the ability to appreciate their parents' struggles.

Wanting to Show Your Parents Appreciation Will Make You a Stronger Person

Your parents work so hard to bring you up, though you may not see it. When you realize how much you owe them and resolve to repay them in some way for all they have done for you, you will be filled with great energy and strength.

When Nichiren Daishonin was twelve years old, he vowed to repay his debt of gratitude to his parents by becoming the "wisest person in all Japan" (WND-1, 175).

Our heart, our intent, is indeed the foundation for everything. If you have even the desire to show your appreciation for your parents, there is no limit to the growth you can achieve.

The next step, of course, is showing appreciation to your parents in some concrete way.

Addressing his youthful disciple Nanjo Tokimitsu, the Daishonin recommends that when you want to give your parents something nice but don't have anything on hand, just give them a smile two or three times a day (see WND-2, 636). This is very clear and simple advice.

As members of the future division,[7] you have yet to enter the workforce, so buying expensive gifts for your parents will only cause them to worry. But smiles don't cost anything. You can withdraw limitless smiles from the bank of your heart. It is a gift that will please your parents most.

A smiling child is a source of unconditional happiness for a loving parent.

How Can I Show My Parents My Appreciation?

For now, being good sons and daughters means studying your hardest and developing yourselves so that eventually you can lead many others to happiness and make a positive contribution to society and the world. For a parent, there is surely no greater pride or joy than to have their child grow into a person who others look up to and appreciate. It makes them feel that all their efforts in raising their child have been rewarded.

The best possible way for you to be good sons and daughters is through your own growth and victory. The parent-child relationship continues no matter what your age. A parent is always a parent, and a child always a child. Even after death, the lives of parent and child remain connected. From that perspective, being good sons and daughters to your parents is a lifelong endeavor. The key is to steadily polish and develop yourselves, without being impatient.

The debt of gratitude owed to one's father and mother is as vast as the ocean. If one cares for them while they are alive, but does nothing to help them in their next life, it will be like a mere drop of water.

—Nichiren

Your Words Are the Magic to Create a Warmer Family

Responding pleasantly when your parents ask you something is important. That's the magic trick for reassuring them. For example, when your parents wish you a good day as they see you off to school, respond with a cheerful, "See you later!" When they ask if you're doing your homework, just say, "Yes, I'm doing it now!" And when they tell you to turn the TV off, call out, "OK, I will in a minute!" Whatever the situation, responding in an upbeat way will put your parents' minds at ease.

The important thing is to try to express your sincere feelings to your parents. Tell them: "I really appreciate you!" "I chant for your good health every day," or "I promise to make you proud and take you on an overseas trip one day!" Just say those kinds of things from time to time. Your parents might be startled and ask if you're running a fever, but they will actually be delighted.

The point is that being good to your parents doesn't have to involve doing something exceptional. Just getting up on time every morning, eating your breakfast, and going to school; studying hard; staying on good terms with your friends—all of those can be ways of being good sons and daughters, since they will reassure your parents and keep them from worrying about you.

Daisaku Ikeda (left) with a fellow student, Tokyo, 1940s. (PHOTO: SEIKYO PRESS)

How to Understand the Truth About Bullies So You Can Better Deal with Them

When I've Tried to Stop People From Bullying Others at School, I Just End Up Getting Bullied Myself. I Don't Want to Be the Kind of Person Who Ignores It, but I Feel Helpless. What Should I Do?

When you cannot get the bullies to stop picking on others through your own efforts, talk to your principal, your homeroom teacher, older students whom you trust, or your parents. Think of some way to improve the situation.

If that doesn't work, pray to the Gohonzon. But whatever happens, you must not get down on yourself if you cannot solve the problem. Even if you find you cannot do or say anything right now, it's important to recognize that bullying is wrong.

Rather than deciding there is something wrong with you, concentrate on developing yourself so that you can effect a positive change in the future. If you end up in a fight and only get beaten up yourself, it won't solve anything. You have to find a long-term solution.

Basically, unless we cultivate an awareness of human rights in society, we cannot begin to prevent abuse.

I Have a Physical Disability. People at School Make Fun of Me. How Should I Handle This?

Essentially, you have to become stronger. That is part of the human rights struggle. Having your rights as a human being recognized by others is not just having people behave sympathetically toward you. Be proud of yourself as an individual, regardless of your disability. You must be proud of your mission.

Those who laugh at you and make fun of you are cruel and wrong. They create a terrible burden of negative karma for themselves by ignoring your right to be treated as a human being.

Letting their taunts get to you is a defeat for human rights. Your strength, however, is a victory for human rights.

Bullying Is War in Miniature

Some have said that bullying is just war in miniature. I remember something that happened during World War II, when I was about your age or maybe a little younger.

A soldier came walking by with a woman. It just happened that an army officer was there too. When the soldier walked past him, the officer shouted, "You didn't salute properly!" and began kicking and beating the soldier viciously.

The soldier had saluted correctly, but the officer seemed jealous that the soldier had a female companion, and he took it out on the poor man. That's why he beat the soldier in front of his girlfriend and a large crowd of people.

The soldier, of course, dared not resist. I will never forget the face of the woman, who was in tears. I remember thinking how much I disliked people who mistreat others. I knew even then that our military was vicious and wrong.

Pettiness, arrogance, jealousy, and self-centeredness—all those base and destructive emotions violate human rights. On a larger scale, they manifest as war and crime.

How to Deal with the
Death of Someone You Care About

Can My Chanting Reach Someone Who Has Died?

The sound of our chanting reaches the lives of those who have entered the state of death. Of course, it also reaches those who are still alive. The power of Nam-myoho-renge-kyo can illuminate anywhere in the universe, even the farthest reaches of the state of hell, filling it with the warm light of hope, peace, and comfort.

Myoho is composed of two Chinese characters, *myo* and *ho*. *Myo*, meaning mystic, or wonderful, symbolizes death and *ho*, meaning law, symbolizes life. Together, as the Mystic Law, they represent the "oneness of life and death," the two phases of our existence. Life and death may seem separate and independent of each other, but within that dynamic exists the identity of our life that is one and unchanging. It continues forever through alternating periods of life and death.

Nam-myoho-renge-kyo is the fundamental rhythm of that eternal life. Chanting Nam-myoho-renge-kyo has the power to help even those in the state of death.

> Death is not the greatest loss in life. The greatest loss is what dies inside us while we live.

Norman Cousins
1915–2000
Journalist, Peace Activist

By Chanting, You Can Remove the Suffering of a Loved One Who Has Died

Life is eternal. Suppose a person dies in pain and suffering. Even after death, that person's life may remain in a state of suffering. It might be likened to someone moaning due to a nightmare while sleeping.

If you chant Nam-myoho-renge-kyo with the deceased person in mind, you can remove the suffering from that person's life and impart ease and joy through the rejuvenating and illuminating power of Nam-myoho-renge-kyo. And since chanting is that powerful, there is no way that it cannot help move in the direction of happiness the lives of your parents and friends who are still with you.

Although I and my disciples may encounter various difficulties, if we do not harbor doubts in our hearts, we will as a matter of course attain Buddhahood.

—Nichiren

Everything That Happens to Us Has Meaning

When Mr. Toda was a young man, he lost one of his children. He once said: "When I was twenty-three, I lost my daughter, Yasuyo. I held my dead child in my arms all through the night. At the time, I had not yet taken faith in the Gohonzon, and I was so grief stricken that I slept with her in my embrace.

"And so we parted, and now I am fifty-eight years old. When she died she was three, so if she were alive now, I imagine she would be a fine woman in the prime of her life. Have I or have I not met my deceased daughter again in this life? This is a matter of one's own perception through faith. I believe that I have met her. Whether one is united with a deceased relative in this life or the next is all a matter of one's perception through faith."

Mr. Toda shared this experience to encourage a member who had lost a young child. He was responding to the member's question, "Is it possible to reestablish a parent-child relationship with my deceased child again in this lifetime?"

After losing his daughter, Mr. Toda also lost his wife. He suffered enormous grief and heartache, but he said it was that very suffering which allowed him now to encourage and comfort others and, as a leader of many people, become the sort of person who understood others' feelings.

Everything that happens to us has a meaning. Though you may be sad and filled with pain to the point it seems unbearable, as long as you keep pressing forward, resolved to never give up or to never be defeated, you will come to see the meaning of that experience. That is the power of faith. It is also the essence of life.

If Someone Dies of an Illness, Is That a Sign of Failure or Weak Faith?

No. A person who has strong and invincible faith to the very end has triumphed. There are many people who, in spite of being fatally ill and suffering greatly themselves, have prayed for kosen-rufu and the happiness of their fellow members and encouraged others right up to the very moment of death. Their lives and their bravery in the face of death have given courage and inspiration to countless others. Such people will be reborn quickly with a healthy body.

I knew a young girl who was found to have a brain tumor when she was eleven. She died at fourteen.

But through it all, she was so cheerful that she even inspired the adults in the hospital. She shared her bright, positive spirit with everyone she met. No doubt her illness caused her terrible pain, but she continued to chant and to encourage others.

Toward the end, she said to one of her visitors: "As for me and my illness, whatever happens is fine. I've stopped praying for

The Venerable Maudgalyayana put his faith in the Lotus Sutra, which is the greatest good there is, and thus not only did he himself attain Buddhahood, but his father and mother did so as well. And, amazing as it may seem, all the fathers and mothers of the preceding seven generations and the seven generations that followed, indeed, of countless lifetimes before and after, were able to become Buddhas.

—Nichiren

myself. There are so many others worse off than me. I pray with all my heart that they will take faith as soon as possible and find out for themselves just how wonderful the Gohonzon is."

To her parents she said: "What if this had happened to you, Dad? We'd be in terrible trouble! And it would be just as bad if it happened to you, Mom. And if it happened to my little brother, I'm sure he couldn't handle it. I'm glad that it happened to me instead of any of you. . . . I'm sure this is the result of a promise I made before I was born. If those who know me learn something from my life, I will be happy."

I heard about this girl's struggle with illness, and I sent her roses. I also sent her a Japanese fan on which I had written the words *Light of Happiness*, as well as a photograph I had taken of a field of irises in bloom. I heard that she was over-joyed when she received them.

The words she left to those around her were "Faith means believing until the very end." And she demon-strated those words with her own life. There was a long, long line of friends and family at her funeral. In her brief fourteen and a half years, she had told more than a thousand people of the greatness of the Mystic Law.

Her name was Akemi Yamada, and she was from Kashiwa City, Chiba Prefecture, Japan. [She died in October 1982.] She won. That is what I feel. Her entire life, and all her suffering, had meaning. Or rather, through her struggle, she gave meaning to her suffering.

Akemi said that her illness was the result of a promise she'd made before she was born. Buddhism teaches the concept of deliberately choosing our circumstances. This means to live based upon the view that we have boldly volunteered to be born into this world beset with suffering so that we might demon-strate the power of Buddhism to others through our struggles and subsequent triumphs. This is the way of life of a bodhisattva.

If those with faith had every advan-tage from the start, people would never know the power of Buddhism.

That is why we have chosen to be born amid troubled circumstances, to show others what it means to do human revolution.

It is like a play, a great drama.

Suicide

Suicide rates are high all around the world. This is an unfortunate, heartbreaking reality. People who kill themselves feel as if they have no way out. They don't have the strength to fight, or anywhere to take refuge or find solace. But seeking escape in death does not end suffering. In fact, by destroying the treasure that is their own life, they commit a grave offense that only adds further to their misery.

Those who commit suicide feel trapped and drained of life force. But such feelings come from living essentially in opposition to the fundamental Law of life, the Mystic Law. The entire universe flows in the rhythm of life and death. The largest star lives and dies, the smallest insect lives and dies. All phenomena move in the rhythm of life and death.

The foundation of all life and death is Nam-myoho-renge-kyo. That is why our life force grows weak if we act counter to the Mystic Law and grows strong if we practice the Mystic Law.

At any rate, suicide is always and absolutely wrong.

A single life is worth more than the major world system. You still have many years ahead of you, and moreover you have encountered the Lotus Sutra. If you live even one day longer, you can accumulate that much more benefit. How truly precious your life is!

—Nichiren

How Having a Mentor Helps You
Lead a Meaningful Life

Strive for Self-Improvement

The path of mentor and disciple is not something out of the ordinary. Just as birds follow the path of birds, and fish follow the path of fish, human beings also have their path.

The path of mentor and disciple enables us to lead the most dignified and meaningful lives and to keep striving for self-improvement.

In fields such as academia, the arts, and sports, there are also mentors who teach the correct path to follow.

Mr. Toda is my mentor because he taught me the path of Buddhism and the correct way to live as a human being.

Have a Spiritual Compass in Our Hearts

Our feelings and emotions are constantly changing—one moment we may feel happy, the next sad; one moment enjoying ourselves, and the next filled with pain. This is especially true during the time of youth.

Nichiren Daishonin cites the words: "Become the master of your mind rather than let your mind master you" (WND-1, 502).

It might seem fun to just do as we please all the time, but if we live our lives ruled by fleeting emotions, we will eventually lose our way. That's why it's so important to have a mentor whose guidance and example we can keep in our hearts as a spiritual compass.

Mr. Toda is always in my heart. To this day, I have an inner dialogue with him every day. I always ask myself what he'd do in my situation and what would make him proud. Because I have this inner foundation, I am never uncertain or afraid.

The path of mentor and disciple is the supreme path of human life. It is a path of justice and a path of hope. It is a path of happiness and victory.

Great Individuals Never Forget Their Mentors

The ancient Greek philosopher Plato (427 BC–347 BC) had Socrates (469 BC–399 BC) for a mentor, and the American civil rights leader Martin Luther King Jr. (1929–68) had Benjamin Mays (1894–1984, president of Morehouse College, King's alma mater).

All the world leaders I have met had mentors whom they were indebted to. They were all great individuals who never forgot their gratitude to the mentors who contributed to their growth.

Genuine mentors seek to foster their disciples or students into capable individuals who go on to surpass them. Disciples who have a good mentor can awaken to and make full use of their innate strengths and abilities.

The renowned Indian poet and educator Rabindranath Tagore (1861–1941) said: "Man knows himself as great where he sees great men."[8] Tagore also had a mentor when he was a student. I would like to dedicate the aforementioned words of his to you, my young friends.

If you can't fly then run, if you can't run then walk, if you can't walk then crawl, but whatever you do you have to keep moving forward.

Martin Luther King Jr.
1929–68
Civil Rights Leader, Minister

PHOTO: DUANE HOWELL/THE DENVER POST VIA GETTY IMAGES

Mentor and Disciple Are Equal

The mentor-disciple relationship is the most fundamental path of life.

In Buddhism, while mentor and disciple are different individuals, their hearts are one. They are also essentially equal. That is what is meant by "oneness of mentor and disciple." Mentor and disciple are one in spirit. As such, they always advance together.

My mentor, Josei Toda, always highly valued the opinions of young people. He listened attentively to what they had to say, and deeply admired their earnest seeking spirit.

He often asked for my views, inquiring: "Daisaku, what do you think? What's your opinion?"

I was always very moved that he would put that much trust in an ordinary young man like myself. I was so grateful to have such a wonderful mentor.

Become Strong and Surpass the Mentor

I wonder if you've ever heard of the expression, "from the indigo, an even deeper blue"? It appears in the writings of Nichiren Daishonin. The color blue is created by dyeing material such as fabric with the pigment of the indigo plant, and through the process of repeatedly soaking the material in the dye, a deeper blue than the original dye can be created. This expression also has the meaning of disciples surpassing their mentor.

To me, you are all my direct disciples who will go on to become "bluer than the indigo."

That's why I would like all of you to become strong and outstanding individuals no matter what, and proudly make your way in the wide world. Because mentor and disciple are one, I have no doubt that you can achieve this.

My eternal message to you all is: "Nothing is impossible for Soka mentors and disciples. The spirit of the future division is to never give up. You can surely triumph!"

Unite in Spirit and Achieve Anything

I continue chanting for you, the future division members, day after day, with faith in your great growth and victory.

Chanting creates the strongest "life waves" possible, as Nichiren Daishonin states: "There is nowhere throughout the worlds of the ten directions that the sound of our voices chanting daimoku [Nam-myoho-renge-kyo] do not reach" (GZ, 808).[9] With this in mind, I hope you'll also chant Nam-myoho-renge-kyo with faith in your own great growth and victory. This is chanting with the shared spirit of mentor and disciple, by which our lives will definitely connect. So even if you lack self-confidence now, there's nothing to worry about. The "sun" of self-confidence is certain to rise in the hearts of those who make efforts.

The Daishonin teaches that if mentor and disciple are united in spirit, they can achieve anything.

You're Never Alone

Of course, when you're young, you may often feel anxious and uncertain. There may be times when you feel frustrated with who you are, or find it hard to believe in yourself. That's perfectly fine. Because remember, I always believe in you more than anyone. I'm watching over you and praying wholeheartedly for you. Please advance cheerfully, with optimism and confidence.

Whatever the time or place, we can always have a dialogue in our hearts. Let's face every problem together, look forward with hope, and advance victoriously together!

I would like every one of you to make your youth a time brimming with great cheer and triumph. Please lead lives of happiness, overflowing with joy. This is the spirit of a mentor, and my wish for all of you.

Each step you take forward will itself become the golden path of mentor and disciple.

Let's set forth! Let's walk the path to victory together!

You

& the

world

The world is your challenge; it is your true stage.

—Josei Toda

How to Contribute to
World Peace (aka "Kosen-rufu")

When We Change, the World Changes

When we change, the world changes. The key to all change is in our inner transformation—a change in our hearts and minds. This is human revolution. We all have the power to change. When we realize this truth of life, we can bring forth that power anywhere, anytime, and in any situation.

Nichiren Buddhism, based on the transformative principles of the Lotus Sutra, has made this great path of inner change available to all people, with the chanting of Nam-myoho-renge-kyo as its core practice.

Peace Starts With Respect for Your Mom and Dad

That beautiful feeling of respect for one's mother is a starting point for peace. The Daishonin says that he launched his great struggle to help all people attain enlightenment in order to repay his debt of gratitude to his mother (see WND-1, 931).

Mothers are great. They are strong, resilient, and gentle. If humanity could always remember the spirit of a mother's love, there would be no more wars. When you cherish your mothers, you are cultivating the spirit of peace.

Please continue to strive and grow for the sake of your mothers. I hope you'll help her with the housework sometimes. At first, your mother may wonder what's going on. But just explain that you're taking your first step toward building peace!

Your mother will be delighted to think that you're an emissary of peace.

And try to be nice to your father too!

The SGI and World Peace

The SGI is an organization working to realize the great objective of kosen-rufu—of achieving peace and happiness for all humanity based on the principles and philosophy of Nichiren Buddhism. Such an objective cannot be accomplished through the efforts of one person alone. It becomes possible only when people in various spheres of society come together, organize themselves into a cohesive force, and work to achieve that goal.

What Does Kosen-rufu Mean and When Will It Actually Happen?

Kosen means to widely declare. "Widely" implies speaking out to the world, to an ever-greater number and ever-broader spectrum of people.

"Declare" means to proclaim one's ideals, principles, and philosophy. The *ru* of *rufu* means a current like that of a great river. And *fu* means to spread out like a roll of cloth.

Kosen-rufu is the spread of the Mystic Law from one person to another. It is also its spread from ten thousand to fifty thousand. Yet, kosen-rufu is not about numbers. It is a process, an eternal flow.

Kosen-rufu will not end at some fixed point in time. We won't sit down one day and say, "Well, now kosen-rufu is finished." Not only would that spell our spiritual death, we'd lose all motivation to do human revolution.

Kosen-rufu is unending. Although we try to describe it by defining certain conditions, in reality, kosen-rufu has no set form.

Peace is not wimpy. It's about sitting down and negotiating with people you hate. Ultimately, all occupation ends, and you have to deal with the enemy.

Betty Williams
1943–
Northern Ireland Peace Activist,
Nobel Peace Prize Winner

It All Starts With You Being Courageous

Only when people have the courage to stand alone can they lead the world in the direction of peace and good. When such courageous individuals join forces in strong solidarity, they can change society. But it all starts with you. You have to be courageous. The rest follows from that.

Fight Against the Use of Nuclear Weapons

Nuclear weapons embody the ultimate form of violence. Back in 1957, my mentor, second Soka Gakkai President Josei Toda, called on us youth to fight against the use of nuclear weapons. He not only insisted that all such weapons of mass destruction must be abolished but taught us about the need to rip out the claws of the demonic nature inherent in human life.

Nichiren says: "Life is the foremost of all treasures. It is expounded that even the treasures of the entire major world system cannot equal the value of one's body and life. Even the treasures that fill the major world system

are no substitute for life" (WND-1, 1125). Our lives are more precious than all the treasures in the universe. The sanctity of life is the basis of Buddhist philosophy. It is vital that more and more people in the world embrace this fundamental belief.

Self-Restraint Is Necessary to Realize Lasting Peace

Peace cannot be a mere stillness, a quiet interlude between wars. It must be a vital and energetic arena of life activity, won through our own volitional, proactive efforts. Peace must be a living drama—in Benedict de Spinoza's (1632–77) words, "a virtue that springs from force of character."[10] Eternal peace is a continuum consciously maintained through the interaction of self-restraining individuals within a self-restraining society. . . .

Political systems aside, what can nurture truthful, nonviolent, and pure-hearted people? The building of lasting peace depends on how many people capable of self-restraint can be fostered through religious practice. If a religion is worthy of the name, and if it can respond to the needs of contemporary times, it should nurture in its followers the spiritual base for becoming good citizens of the world.

Buddhism teaches that the ultimate objective of the Buddha's life was revealed in the humanity he manifested in his behavior and actions. Thus the cultivation and perfection of a person's character are considered in the Buddhist tradition to be the true goals of religious training.

Your Victories Are the Hope of the World

America is a land of freedom. But along with the sometimes dizzying freedom that can be found there, there is also a deep, impenetrable darkness. America is a microcosm of the world. This is where you live.

In a way, we could say that your problems represent the problems of all humanity. In that respect, your victory will open the way to victory for the youth of the entire world. It will also illuminate the path along which humanity must advance in the twenty-first century. You are the hope of America and the world!

We Must Fight Against the Trend Toward Isolation

People today seem more isolated and disconnected, and human ties are increasingly growing weaker.

Human beings need one another to survive. No matter how tough one tries to act in being alone, a lonely life is sad and unhappy. It doesn't bring a true sense of happiness.

If the number of isolated youth increases, society, too, will invariably face many problems. Now, more than ever, a philosophy that unites people and dialogue that forges heart-to-heart connections are essential for leading truly rich and fulfilling lives.

It always seems impossible until it is done.

Nelson Mandela
1918–2013
Anti-apartheid Revolutionary,
South Africa's
First Black President

Addressing Spiritual Homelessness

In America, the homeless problem has become a serious social dilemma. Homeless people are said to number in the millions. But I fear that the number of spiritually homeless people is even greater. These people go about searching for a comfortable place, their house of the soul, or spiritual home. The power of Buddhism provides people with a place of essential tranquillity, a sweet home of life. Nichiren Daishonin states: "No place is secure. Be convinced that Buddhahood is the final abode" (WND-1, 491).

From the outset, America has been a country to which people from around the world have flocked, leaving their homelands for one reason or another. They came to this country searching for a new home. It is the task of our movement to breathe life into America's purpose of building a new home for these people. Society will become a genuine home to all only when it provides each person with absolute peace and compassionate protection.

Flint has the potential to produce fire, and gems have intrinsic value. We ordinary people can see neither our own eyelashes, which are so close, nor the heavens in the distance. Likewise, we do not see that the Buddha exists in our own hearts.

—Nichiren

How to Understand &
Appreciate the SGI

The SGI Exists for People, Not the Other Way Around

The organization of the Soka Gakkai emerged naturally from the spirit to somehow encourage another person, to want to see others become happy. The Soka Gakkai didn't appear first and then become filled with people. People began forging bonds with one another, and then those ties of friendship spread, naturally giving birth to the Soka Gakkai organization. For that reason, we must be aware that the organization exists for people. People don't exist for the organization. Please never forget this point.

I hope you will give your lives to being the staunchest friends and supporters of those suffering or in distress. And I hope you will cherish the Soka Gakkai, an organization of and for the people—that

you will revere it, support it, and work for its development. This is my heartfelt request of all of you.

What if I Don't Like Certain Aspects of the SGI?

When I was still a new member, I did not like the Soka Gakkai as it was at that time. I could not accept the behavior and bearing of my seniors. Learning of my honest feelings, President Toda said to me: "If that's how you feel, Daisaku, then what you have to do is make the Soka Gakkai into the kind of organization you can be truly happy with. Work really hard and fight earnestly to build a Soka Gakkai that matches your ideal!"

His answer was extremely clear; it also showed his incredible broad-mindedness and generosity. Following my mentor's words,

I subsequently went on to build a new Soka Gakkai.

The SGI's Purpose: Mobilizing Human Goodness

Our organization exists to mobilize such human goodness—people's desire to help and benefit others—and use it to create great value. You might say the Soka Gakkai is a body or organism that took form and came to life specifically to bring together the basic goodness of people's hearts, to further develop that goodness and strengthen it. Without the organization, there would be no cohesion or order to our efforts.

An organization dedicated to good enhances people's capacity to work for good and promotes unlimited growth and self-improvement. It does not hinder people's progress or lead them astray. It supports people's self-development, putting them on a sure course to happiness and personal growth. And it is for this purpose that our organization exists.

In that respect, the organization is a means. The end, meanwhile, is for people to become happy.

I Don't Like Organizations in General Because I Don't Like to Be Told What to Do. So Why Should I Be a Part of the SGI?

Organizations that deprive people of their freedom and identity definitely do exist. They exploit people to achieve their own objectives. This is a negative aspect that organizations can have.

However, though you may dislike organizations, is remaining alone really a sign of freedom? Can you guarantee that you won't lose sight of yourself anyway? That's hard to say. Genuine freedom does not mean living selfishly and doing just as you please; it is traveling the correct path in life.

The earth, for example, revolves around the sun. If it were to stray from its orbit even in the slightest, it would spell disaster. A spacecraft, if it assumes the correct course, can traverse the vast cosmos and reach its destination. This is the meaning of true freedom.

Human Relations Help Us Grow

Our organization is one of great human diversity. This acts as a stimulus for our personal growth. In many sports, it's hard to assess your real ability if you train or practice only by yourself. We develop and grow through contact with many other people. In Japan, the mountain potatoes known as taro are rough and dirty when harvested, but when placed together in a basin of running water and rolled against one another, the skin is peeled away, leaving them shining clean and ready for cooking. It's probably inappropriate to compare people to potatoes, but my point is that the only way for us to hone and polish our character is through our interactions with others.

Being on your own without having to see or think about others may seem very comfortable and hassle free, but you'll find yourself locked in a world that is terribly small and limited. If you avoid belonging to any group or organization, you deprive yourself of contact with many people and, in the end, you are left wondering about the meaning of your existence.

Just as flowers open up and bear fruit, just as the moon appears and invariably grows full, just as a lamp becomes brighter when oil is added, and just as plants and trees flourish with rain, so will human beings never fail to prosper when they make good causes.

—Nichiren

Unity—Not Division— Is What Is Needed

The devilish workings of egoism inherent in human life create barriers that divide people. In contrast, the positive workings of the Buddha or our innate Buddhahood—manifesting as respect for the individual and the dignity of life—sweep away those barriers and bring people together.

During the Cold War, which had erected a massive barrier between the Eastern and Western blocs, Mr. Toda taught us to start our efforts for world peace from our immediate environment and actively engage in dialogue to help break down the walls dividing people.

Today, the world faces numerous problems, including global environmental issues, regional conflicts, poverty, and social inequality. These problems cannot be solved by one person or by one country, nor can they be solved by international political and economic policies alone. Now more than ever, we need the united power of the people to surmount all barriers. This is the only hope for effecting positive change in today's world.

We need the united power of the people to surmount all barriers. (PHOTO: JEREMY JOFFEE)

It's Nearly Impossible to Practice Buddhism by Ourselves

Why do we practice Nichiren Buddhism? We practice in order to build an unshakable self, like a towering mountain, so that we can fearlessly surmount all hardships and struggles. This is what it means to attain Buddhahood in this lifetime. However, in the Latter Day that is rife with negative influences, it's nearly impossible to carry out our Buddhist practice successfully just by ourselves.

The Daishonin states: "When a tree has been transplanted, though fierce winds may blow, it will not topple if it has a firm stake to hold it up. . . . Even a feeble person will not stumble if those supporting him are strong, but a person of considerable strength, when alone, may fall down on an uneven path" (WND-1, 598). Having good friends who support us is essential to upholding correct faith to the very end and leading lives of genuine victory. The Soka Gakkai is a realm of "good friends" of the kind described by the Daishonin.

Hope for All Humanity

There are people who criticize and attack our organization. But are they the ones who will teach others how to achieve absolute happiness? No, they are not. Those who recognized this encouraged one another to become happy and came together to help those who were suffering. And the result is the Soka Gakkai. This is a fact most solemn and sublime. The organization is the crystallization of genuine democracy, handmade by the people, for the people. It is the only body carrying out the widespread propagation of Nichiren Buddhism, which places the highest value on the dignity of the human being. It is the sun of hope for all humanity. That is why President Toda declared that the Soka Gakkai organization was more precious than his life. I feel exactly the same way.

SGI Meetings Help Us Move Our Lives Forward

At SGI meetings, we can hear others' experiences in faith. Members share their triumphant stories of overcoming problems through their Buddhist practice. People are making positive efforts to move forward in their lives, chanting Nam-myoho-renge-kyo, and refusing to be defeated by obstacles. When someone is struggling or going through some problem, we warmly support and encourage them like family, letting them know we are there for them and chanting for their happiness. These gatherings of good, sincere people are truly unique in the world.

Faith means putting one's trust in the Lotus Sutra . . . as parents refuse to abandon their children, or as a child refuses to leave its mother.

—Nichiren

How to:
Become a Global Citizen

Our Spirit and Actions Are What Make Us Global Citizens

Have you heard the expression, "Think globally, act locally"? That is the essential requirement for becoming a global citizen.

The American futurist Hazel Henderson, with whom I have engaged in a dialogue, made this her slogan in her efforts to confront global environmental problems. In our dialogue, she said that it is not difficult to be a global citizen, and that in trying to solve global problems, we should do whatever we can in the place where we are right now as fellow inhabitants of planet Earth.

I hope you will all take her words to heart.

What makes us global citizens is our spirit, and also the actions we take on a daily basis.

Learn Foreign Languages

When I was your age, Japan was at war. English was regarded as an "enemy language," and we were not allowed to study it. I always think that if I could go back to my student days, I would try to become proficient in a foreign language. That's why I hope you will learn many foreign languages while you are still young and make friends all around the world. Then, if you have the chance, please take your parents overseas as well.

Worldwide kosen-rufu was Nichiren Daishonin's lifelong dream. In his writings, there are many references to "Jambudvipa," which means "the entire world."

As young people who uphold and practice the great teaching of Nichiren Buddhism, you are all certain to take your place on the world stage as inspiring global citizens and make wonderful contributions as leaders of society and kosen-rufu.

SGI Members Are Global Citizens

All of you have the perfect example of global citizenship right in front of you—in the form of your parents and your fellow SGI members who practice Nichiren Buddhism. They work tirelessly day after day for the well-being of others and their communities, as well as being passionately committed to the great ideal of worldwide kosen-rufu. When they come across someone who is suffering, they share the SGI's inspiring life philosophy with them, explain the Law of the universe, and share personal experiences of revitalizing their lives through their Buddhist practice. They empathize with others, chant with them, and encourage them wholeheartedly. None can match their tenacious and steadfast dedication to the happiness of humanity and world peace.

If you care anything about your personal security, you should first of all pray for order and tranquillity throughout the four quarters of the land, should you not?

—Nichiren

How to Appreciate
Art & Culture as a Force for Good

The Aim of True Art and Culture

True art, true culture, strives to enrich the individual and encourage self-expression, while seeking to reach out, touch, communicate, and bring people together. It arises from the spirit to bring joy to others and not from a desire for fame or profit.

Art Can Be Found in Our Daily Activities

Many of our daily activities resonate with the spirit of art and culture. For instance, when we try to look our best, we are seeking to create beauty. When we tidy and clean a room, we are striving to create beauty. Just one flower in a vase can completely transform a room, giving it a warm and gentle touch. Such is the power of beauty.

I Feel a Little Put Off by Art. How Can I Come to Appreciate It?

To begin by simply enjoying art is most important. If you start out with a scholarly or analytical approach, you're likely to end up confused and in the dark about what art really is. I doubt very much that people listening to a bird's song or gazing at a meadow of flowers analyze such beauty intellectually.

Of course, to fully appreciate some great artworks, one needs to concentrate and make a degree of mental effort. But appreciation starts with simply experiencing the work. With music, for instance, we begin by just listening. With a painting, we start by looking.

How to Create Great Art

Great art is infused with powerful vital force. It is alive, endowed with the creator's life and spirit. The renowned French sculptor Auguste Rodin (1840–1917) said that the important thing for artists is to feel, to love, to hope, to tremble, to live. It is to be, before an artist, he said, a human being. These human feelings—hope, love, anger, fear—are communicated to us through the artist's work. The vibrations of the artist's spirit set off similar vibrations within our hearts. This is the essential experience of art. It is a shared feeling that links the creator and the viewer, transcending boundaries of time and space.

Art Can Set Our True Selves Free

Life is painful. It has thorns, like the stem of a rose. Culture and art are the roses that bloom on that stem.

The institutions of society tend to treat us as parts in a machine. They assign us ranks and place considerable pressure upon us to fulfill our defined roles. We need something to help us restore our lost and distorted humanity. Each of us has feelings that have been suppressed and have built up inside. We have a voiceless cry resting in the depths of our souls, waiting for expression. Art gives those feelings voice and form.

> As a day well spent brings happy sleep, so a life well used brings happy death?

Leonardo da Vinci
1452–1519
Artist, Scientist, "Renaissance Man"

We can also vent those feelings through pleasures and play, which may suffice for a while, but in the long run such distractions bring no true satisfaction or sense of fulfillment. Our lives will grow dull and lusterless, we will feel empty inside, because our true selves, our true hearts' desires, have not been set free at the deepest core. Art is the cry of the soul from the core of one's being.

Creating and appreciating art set free the soul trapped deep within us. That is why art causes such joy. Art, quite aside from any questions of skill or its lack, is the emotion, the pleasure of expressing one's life exactly as it is. Those who see such art are moved by its passion, its strength, its intensity, and its beauty. That is why it is impossible to separate a fully human life from art.

Second Soka Gakkai President Josei Toda makes his declaration calling for the abolition of nuclear weapons, Yokohama, Japan, September 8, 1957. (PHOTO: SEIKYO PRESS)

How to Be a Great Leader so We can Get This
World Peace Party Started

True Leaders Make the People Wise

Generally speaking, we can see two approaches to being a leader of people. One is to make the people wise. The other is to keep them ignorant. This is the difference between true leadership and dictatorship.

Those Who Have Suffered Can Make Great Leaders

How can those who have never suffered understand the feelings of the people? How can they endure hardship after hardship to achieve something great? If people who haven't suffered become leaders, everyone under them will be the worse for it. I don't want to let that happen to the Soka Gakkai.

The same principle holds true for our nation and our world. The task of leaders is to take care of those who are suffering the most. When people have leaders who don't understand this point, they are doomed to misfortune.

You Must Lead the Way

You, today's youth, are the new leaders of a new age. You must create a history of human unity for the dawning of this new age on our planet. Perhaps you think that there is little you can do as individuals. But, as Victor Hugo (1802–85) observed, "An invasion of armies can be resisted; an invasion of ideas cannot be resisted."[11] We are moving toward an ever-expanding humanism.

I am convinced that whatever twists and turns there may be along the way, that is the direction. You, my young friends, embracing a philosophy of humanism for which the world so hungers, are the front-runners who will lead the way.

The future has several names. For the weak, it is impossible; for the fainthearted, it is unknown; but for the valiant, it is ideal.

Victor Hugo
1802–85
Poet, Novelist, Playwright

PHOTO: DEAGOSTINI/GETTY IMAGES

You Must Read the Classics to Be a Leader of Character

You cannot imagine how strict Mr. Toda was when it came to reading. Seeing youth engrossed in tabloid publications, he would become furious, sternly rebuking them: "How can you enjoy that garbage? Do you want to be nothing more than a third- or fourth-rate person? You must read epic novels, you must read the classics! You can never hope to forge your character if you don't read them while you are young! You will never become a leader in the future!"

Mr. Toda was also always checking on me, asking, "What are you reading now?" If I were to answer, "Rousseau's *Émile*," for example, he would ask me about the content—there was no way I could pretend to have read something I hadn't!

Even just two weeks before he died, Mr. Toda was still inquiring about my reading. He said: "A leader must never forget the importance of reading, no matter what may happen. I'm up to the third volume of the ancient Chinese work *Compendium of Eighteen Histories*." Even in his weakened physical state, Mr. Toda devoted every spare moment to reading and contemplation.

History Can Be a Guide to Leaders

President Toda always said that leaders should study and read books on history. History helps us see the direction in which society and the world are heading, how we can steer the times in the best direction.

Stand-Out Quality of Great World Leaders

I have met hundreds of world leaders, many of whom are truly excellent and very capable people. Those who stand out in my mind are leaders not driven by ego but those whose lives shine with an invincible spirit to devote themselves to humanity.

Why a Railroad Engineer Was a President's Guest of Honor

I once heard the following story: In the nineteenth century, the president of France was invited to a banquet sponsored by a wealthy countryman. Strangely enough, the French leader found himself seated not as the guest of honor but sixteenth from the head of the table. A railroad engineer occupied the first seat; a literary scholar, the second; and a science professor sat in the third.

A guest, puzzled by the seating order, asked the host why. The response was: "The guests have been seated according to their true importance. By people of true importance, I mean those who possess an outstanding ability and cannot be replaced by anyone else." In other words, because the guest of honor was the world's foremost authority on trains, he was irreplaceable. The guests occupying the second and third seats were also leading experts in their fields. The president, however, could be replaced: Someone else could take over his job.

Whether this story is true or not, it takes a truly mature society to openly spread such frank, candid ideas.

I want you, the high school division members, to become people who support society not in name but in substance. I also hope you will create a society that cherishes such people.

What Is the Root Cause of the World's Problems?

How we view life—the perspective we have on life, on death, on the human condition—is the basis for everything.

Japan today is in deep darkness. It has reached a deadlock, as has much of the rest of the world. What is the root cause of this?

It is a distorted understanding of the fundamental question of life and death. Society's leaders and the majority of people have avoided thinking about this most important of issues, brushing it aside in the pursuit of immediate wants and desires. And we are now seeing the consequences of this negligence. Therefore, if we do not turn our attention to the fundamental issue of life and death, nothing will ever really change. No matter what superficial measures we may take, it will be comparable to trying to treat an illness with pain relievers without addressing the cause. Though our symptoms may temporarily ease, we are only deceiving our bodies, and we will not get better.

The British historian Arnold J. Toynbee (1889–1975) held that the cause of the world's misfortune is that leaders in all fields fail to ponder the basic question of death.

The supreme accomplishment is to blur the line between work and play.

Arnold J. Toynbee
1889-1975
Historian

PHOTO: FRANK SCHERSCHEL/THE LIFE PICTURE COLLECTION/GETTY IMAGES

How to Better Understand the
Causes & Cures of Violence

I Was Physically Attacked. While My Body Is Healing, I Feel Like My Soul May Never Be the Same

Victims of violence are often deeply hurt spiritually as well as physically. They lose trust in their humanity and often feel tarnished as if their lives have been destroyed. If you were a victim of violence, please remember that, no matter what, your value as an individual will never change. Brace yourself firmly. Say to yourself, "I am not a person who will allow such an incident to destroy my life." No one can destroy your life on the deepest level. No matter how much you may have been hurt, you can retain your fundamental dignity—no one can take that from you without your consent.

Buddhism teaches the principle that the pure white lotus grows out of a muddy pond. Likewise, a supreme state of life can grow while living amidst the most painful reality.

No matter how down you may feel, there is someone somewhere suffering in a similar manner, and you in particular can help that person because of your common understanding. And there is the true affection in others' hearts that especially you can discover. You may not feel much like relating your troubles to others, but to have even one person you can consult with about your experiences will make all the difference in your outlook. You should not suffer all by yourself. There is incredible potential inherent within your life. If you should give up on yourself, it would be all the more terrible, because it would amplify the damage already done. Never let your suffering cause you to desert your true self.

It may seem strange, but those who have suffered the most or who have been saddened the most can become the happiest. With the tears you shed, you can cleanse your life and make it shine. Forging ahead is the essence of living and the Buddhist spirit.

Many Young People Are Becoming Violent. Some Are Even Proud of It. How Do We Stop This Trend?

I understand that following the Colorado tragedy at Columbine High School (1999), in which thirteen people were shot to death, President Clinton said, "We must reach out to our children and teach them to express their anger and to resolve their conflicts with words, not weapons." I fully agree. Nothing makes my heart ache more than the fact that young people, who possess infinite potential for the future, destroy their own lives and those of others.

While of course it is vital to control the external elements of violence by abolishing weapons, developing more adequate laws, and establishing peace agreements among nations, ultimately what's needed is to understand that violence arises from an innate human condition. Buddhism terms this condition animality, a state where one is swayed by instinctive desires and has no sense of reason or morality. Even if we may have wiped out all the weapons from this planet, violence will never perish unless we successfully control the animality within us. For this very reason, we need to change the human condition from within.

I have often called for something like a humanitarian competition, where all religions that teach tolerance and concern compete to see how many caring individuals they can each foster. In any case, education based on the dignity of each individual is the key.

Violence is an absolute evil. No matter how correct what you say is, if you resort to violence to prove it, you are a loser. Even if you appear to triumph as a result of violent action, you will end up losing.

Buddhism stresses the interconnectedness of all life. It is only the limited capacity of our senses that causes us to place so much stock in the separation between "them" and "us." Because of this interconnectedness, by using violence, you not only injure or destroy the other person but also yourself. Those who use violence and devalue others' lives actually devalue themselves and ruin their own lives.

It's important to understand that the essence of violence is cowardice. Because a person is cowardly, he or she turns to violence. This individual lacks the courage to have dialogue. Mahatma Gandhi said eloquently that "Non-violence is not a cover for cowardice, but it is the supreme virtue of the brave. . . . Cowardice is wholly inconsistent with non-violence. . . . Non-violence presupposes the ability to strike."[12]

The ability to dialogue is proof of one's intellect. Of course, the top leaders of the nation are mainly responsible for the plight of modern society where violence is common. Adults in the fields of politics, education, and the media share the blame. There is no other way than for you to stand up individually, believing that your efforts can contribute to building a different society from now on. You can start by enlarging the nonviolent circle in your immediate environment.

As we each become able to cherish our own lives, we will naturally be able to value others' lives as well.

The important thing is that you do something. Starting is the first step. Zero is zero even if multiplied by other numbers. But as the saying in Asia goes, "One is the mother of ten thousand."

Violence Toward Women Must Not Be Tolerated

Nothing is so vulgar as violence toward women. Violence must not be tolerated. All men should remember this, and they should look upon their female contemporaries as sisters whose lives are to be cherished. Shame on men if they are not gentle.

At the same time, it is crucial for women to protect themselves with wisdom and prudence. Many groups exist to help women. When you realize how precious your life is, you'll do everything possible to protect it. It is also very important to heed the advice of parents and friends you can trust.

Valuing Life Is the Opposite of Violence

All life is equally precious. We cannot apply a hierarchy of value to life, making one living thing more worthy than another. Each life is unique and individual. Every person's life is as valuable as the universe—it is one with the life of the universe and just as important. Nichiren Daishonin declares, "Life is the foremost of all treasures" (WND-1, 1125). He also states:

"The Buddha says that life is something that cannot be purchased even for the price of an entire major world system" (WND-1, 983) and "One day of life is more valuable than all the treasures of the major world system" (WND-1, 955).

That is why we must never take our own lives. That is why we must not resort to violence, why we must not hurt or bully others. No one has the right to harm the precious treasure that is life.

SGI President Ikeda continues to encourage members around the world through his many writings about Buddhist practice in the modern world. (PHOTO: SEIKYO PRESS)

How to
Protect the Environment

Don't Live at Odds With Nature

Buddhism explains life in a system of ten stages or states of being known as the Ten Worlds—the states of hell, hunger, animality, anger, humanity, heaven, voice-hearers (learning), cause-awakened ones (realization), bodhisattvas, and Buddhahood. The state of humanity is right in the middle, with nobler states of life above and uglier states below. Those states below are unnatural states of being, states at odds with nature. The four stages above humanity all value nature and strive to create a paradise where its beauty flourishes in abundance.

The question is, will we allow ourselves to be dragged down to the lower states, or will we advance to the higher states? Only intelligence, culture, and religious faith can lead us out of the baseness that thoughtlessly consumes nature, leaving a barren wasteland. Because of the "oneness of life and its environment," a desolate, destructive heart or mind produces a desolate, devastated natural environment. The desertification of our planet is linked to the desertification of the human spirit.

Don't Toss Away Your Humanity

Only someone who lives in the selfish state of animality could throw trash or aluminum cans by the road. This is an egoism that cares nothing for others. It is an unnatural way to live. A person who loves nature is simply unable to litter. Tossing one's trash away carelessly is to toss away one's humanity.

Buddhism Is Based on Profound Reverence for Life

The essential teaching of Buddhism is that the life of the Buddha resides in every plant and tree, even in the smallest speck of dust. No philosophy has a more profound reverence for life.

We Have a Duty to Preserve Nature

Government must be dedicated to the good of the people. It is a tragedy that the beautiful natural environment people have cherished and protected for generations is being destroyed in the name of economic growth, political advantage, and scientific progress. Because human beings have the capacity to be aware of the balance of nature, it is our duty to work to preserve it.

PHOTO: CBS VIA GETTY IMAGES

Those who contemplate the beauty of the earth find reserves of strength that will endure as long as life lasts.

Rachel Carson
1907–64
Marine Biologist, Pioneer of the Environmental Movement

How to Learn from History to Make
Your Life WAY Better

The More Problems You Have, the More You Should Study History

Don't get tied in knots over unimportant things. The more problems you have, the more you should read history. Studying history takes you back to the events and lives you are reading about. You meet passionate revolutionaries and base traitors. You encounter vainglorious tyrants and tragic heroes. You come to know people who sought only to lead peaceful lives but were forced to go through difficulties in their lives. You experience the brief moments of peace between seemingly endless stretches of war, like sweet shade from the burning sun.

You see large numbers of people sacrificed for what we now know was foolish superstition, as well as men and women of principle who gave their lives for the love of humanity. You meet great people who pulled themselves up from the depths of suffering to make the impossible possible. You watch this unfolding drama from a distance, or view it as if in its midst—history is played out inside the human mind.

Watching this drama unfold in our minds, we naturally learn to see life from an expansive point of view. We can see ourselves riding the crest of the grand river of history. We see where we have come from, where we are, and where we're going.

History is our roots. Those who have studied history in depth have become aware of their origins, their heritage. Knowing history is knowing oneself. At the same time, the better one knows oneself and human nature, the more accurate picture one gets of history. This is how we acquire an insight into history.

What Can I Gain From Studying History?

One important thing is a broader point of view. If we're always looking at the ground when we walk down the street, we're likely to get lost. But by looking up, choosing something big by which to orient ourselves, we can make sure we are heading in the right direction.

Another way of thinking of it is to imagine yourself looking down from a high mountain. From an elevated vantage point, it is easy to pick out the road on which to proceed.

The same is true of life. If you always have a shallow perspective and only pay attention to trivial things, you are sure to get bogged down in petty concerns and not be able to move forward. Even relatively minor hurdles or problems will seem insurmountable. But if you look at life from a broad viewpoint, you will naturally discover the solution for any problem you confront. This is true when we consider our personal problems as well as those of society and even the future of the world.

History Can Be Interpreted Multiple Ways

History is never definitive. It can be interpreted in many different ways, which is why we mustn't simply accept everything that is written in history books.

For example, let's look at the Crusades launched by Christians in Europe, primarily against Muslims during the Middle Ages. European and Islamic accounts of the Crusades have almost nothing in common! And most of the world history we study in Japan derives from European accounts. Though it's natural if you think about it, Islamic history books don't use the heroic-sounding term *crusader* to describe the aggressors who invaded their lands.

In fact, at the time, Islamic civilization was far more advanced than that of Europe. The crusaders invaded Islamic states, looting and pillaging, leaving a trail of destruction. At least that is how Muslims see it. Islamic histories record the horrible atrocities that the crusaders committed.

The true history of the Crusades is not simply a matter of the past, either. A strong prejudice against Islamic civilization persists today, casting a dark shadow over our chances for world peace. It is a problem of today. It is a problem of the future.

Seek the Truth and Remain Objective

In reading a work of history, you must cultivate your historical sense by always remaining critically aware, by searching for the truth. Sometimes you will agree with the writer, sometimes not. There is no simple method to achieve this sense of history.

The only way is to study many things, think about many things, and experience many things. And it is crucial to remain objective. You must always seek the facts, the truth, without succumbing to personal biases or self-interest. Never accept a lie.

You Can Make History!

Jawaharlal Nehru (1889–1964), the first prime minister of independent India, said that to read about history is enjoyable, but it is even more exciting to participate in making history oneself.

History is like a chain linking people together. The accomplishments of those who make history have an influence that goes beyond the times in which they were achieved. Great achievements inspire admiration in people of future generations; they also inspire many to take action.

When we take action, we inspire further action—just as our dreams can inspire others to have dreams. Therefore, let us continue to make history in the present.

> If what you have done yesterday still looks big to you, you haven't done much today.

Mikhail Gorbachev
1931–
President and Reformer of the Soviet Union, Nobel Peace Prize Winner

How to
Be a Hero of Justice

Not Doing Good = Doing Bad

Tsunesaburo Makiguchi was strict with people who lacked courage and just stood by and did nothing. The good but fainthearted, in failing to fight evil, are ultimately defeated by it. Mr. Makiguchi often said: "Not doing good is effectively the same as doing bad. Let's say someone places a huge boulder in the middle of the road. This is malicious, as it will cause trouble for those who pass by later. Then someone comes along and sees the large obstruction but, while knowing that it will cause serious problems, leaves it there with the attitude 'Well, I didn't put it there.' This may seem like simply not doing a good thing, but actually, not moving the boulder is causing the same inconvenience for future passersby as putting it there in the first place."

PHOTO: SEIKYO PRESS

> The practical consequences of failing to do good are no different from those of doing evil.

Tsunesaburo Makiguchi
1871–1944
Educator, First Soka Gakkai President

Why Does It Seem That Evil People Have All of the Power and Good People Just Suffer?

Your mission, my young friends, is to change that.

Seven hundred years ago, the three martyrs of Atsuhara—loyal followers of Nichiren who refused to recant their faith—were falsely accused of crimes and executed by priests hostile to Nichiren and in league with the political authorities of the day. Those attached to power are always envious and resentful of the good and just. It is an instinctive, primitive response on the part of those who wish to protect themselves and their own interests at all costs. Another thing is that corrupt people join forces with others of their kind easily and have not the slightest scruple in doing so.

Good people, on the other hand, don't form alliances so easily. The ideal we must aim for is a world in which good people can join hands and work together.

"I don't care what happens to anyone else, as long as I'm OK"—this is the kind of thinking that rationalizes the existence of nuclear weapons. It is an evil way of thinking. And that applies to both nations and individuals.

The crucial question is this: Are you going to ally yourself with evil or good? With wrong or right? Which road will you take in life?

The wise may be called human, but the thoughtless are no more than animals.

—Nichiren

Why Are Good People Persecuted for Standing Up for What Is Right?

Precisely because one upholds what is right, one is persecuted. This is an important concern, past and present, relevant to all countries of the world. Until humanity as a whole has fundamentally transformed itself, this incomprehensible, illogical, yet very real situation will continue. We must face this dark reality. I hope each of you will think about this problem—about the actual examples of it you encounter.

Josei Toda (left) with Tsunesaburo Makiguchi, c. 1930. (PHOTO: SEIKYO PRESS)

Abraham Lincoln (1809–68), president of the United States during the Civil War, abolished slavery and then was assassinated. Though, of course, it was right to work for the equality of African Americans, he was persecuted and killed for it.

Mahatma Gandhi of India rose up against colonial power that oppressed the Indian people. He opposed the high tax on salt, a daily necessity for even the poorest people, and was imprisoned on several occasions. Even though he always acted in the best interests of the people, he was, like Lincoln, assassinated.

Tsunesaburo Makiguchi and Josei Toda fought for what was right, opposing militarism because it caused the people terrible suffering, and yet they, too, were persecuted. Mr. Makiguchi died in prison.

History chronicles the stories of thousands of individuals who were persecuted for doing what was right. And there are countless people whose names have not been remembered but waged similar struggles.

Don't Tolerate Evil

Both good and evil exist in the world. If the people tolerate evil, good will languish and decline. Evil always tries to conceal its true nature. But if we exercise keen powers of discernment, relentlessly pursue and attack evil, and lose no time in confronting it with one question after another, its false skin—its veneer of goodness and justice—will crack and fall away.

How Does Right and Wrong Apply to My Life While I'm in School?

Well, in school, the right thing is to study. And the wrong is to prevent others from studying, or to engage in acts such as vandalizing school property. The purpose of school is study, so the right thing to do is direct your energies toward that end. To be selfish and, simply because you don't like to study, hinder other students or vandalize property is wrong and bad.

It is also wrong to witness evil or injustice and stand by in silence. In cases like that, good people should join forces to prevent bad acts such as bullying.

PHOTO: ANN RONAN PICTURES/
PRINT COLLECTOR/GETTY IMAGES

The best way to find yourself is to lose yourself in the service of others.

Mahatma Gandhi
1869–1948
Leader of India's Independence Movement

How to Create a World That Respects
Human Rights

Buddhism and Human Rights

Buddhism expounds a great, undifferentiating wisdom—the recognition and insight that all living beings are equal, that the Buddha and living beings are one. The highest state of being, Buddhahood, resides in all people. That is why our every effort must be for people and why everything depends on people. Human rights are the distillation of this essential truth.

Every sphere of human endeavor—education, culture, science, government, business, and economics—will either guarantee and foster human rights or come to a dead end. In education, for example, schools should exist for the sake of the students. Yet today, it is as if the students exist for the sake of the schools.

We need to refocus on the importance of benefiting humanity and make a fresh departure from there. That is how human rights will be established.

All Facets of Society Must Teach Human Rights

Those unable to see people of other countries as human beings the same as themselves are spiritually impoverished. They have no sound philosophy of life. They do not ponder life's more profound questions.

They care only for their own petty concerns. Our society is filled with people who are consumed by hunger and at the mercy of unrestrained greed and animality, picking on the weak and fawning on the strong. These negative tendencies are what make our society discriminate against people and ignore human rights.

We must teach all people to see both themselves and others first and foremost as human beings. We have to raise people's awareness of human rights through education. Our schools must teach human rights, our religions must teach human rights, and our government must respect human rights.

Unless we can build a society that regards human beings not as a means to an end but as the end itself, we will remain forever a society of discrimination, unhappiness, and inequality—a realm of animality where the strong prey upon the weak. We will simply repeat the same patterns.

Nichiren Called for Equality of the Sexes Hundreds of Years Ago

To deny equality is to deny the Lotus Sutra.

The Daishonin writes, "There should be no discrimination among those who propagate the five characters of Myoho-renge-kyo in the Latter Day of the Law, be they men or women" (WND-1, 385).

The letter in which this passage appears was written more than seven hundred years ago, in May 1273. In the feudal era of the Middle Ages, the Daishonin was already expounding the equality of the sexes based on the Law.

Looking at gender equality on a worldwide scale, though, it is not until the seventeenth and eighteenth centuries that the concept of the equality of the sexes gained prominence, while it is only in the nineteenth century that women's suffrage movements began to emerge. And it is much later that women actually obtained equal voting rights on par with men in national elections. Women's suffrage was first won in New Zealand in 1893. It was won by the United Kingdom in 1918, the United States in 1920, and Japan in 1945.

This history only serves to bring home again how far ahead of his time the Daishonin was. As early as the thirteenth century, he expounded the equality of the sexes, revealing the profound nature of the egalitarian and humanistic principles of Buddhism.

You Must Respect Yourself Before Others Can Respect You

Rosa Parks (1913–2005) fought against racial discrimination in the United States. She is another of these gentle yet strong people I have met. Even at the height of discrimination against African Americans, she refused to ride in the elevators marked "Colored." Unable to compromise with such discrimination, she took the stairs. She disliked riding on the buses where the seating was segregated and often chose to walk long distances instead.

One hot summer day, although her throat was parched, she went thirsty rather than drink from the "Colored" water fountain. Mrs. Parks writes: "I have never allowed myself to be treated as a second-class citizen. You must respect yourself before others can respect you."[13]

One must live with dignity. Character is the foundation of human rights. It is far more valuable than money.

No true peace can be achieved as long as we seek only material wealth.

We must make the twenty-first century a century of human rights. We must build a society with more than short-term profit as a goal. To do that, the first step is respecting ourselves, living with dignity, self-confidence, and pride. Such

Each person must live their life as a model for others.

Rosa Parks
1913–2005
Civil Rights Activist

PHOTO: MICKEY ADAIR/GETTY IMAGES

people can then treat others with respect. A great river begins with a tiny drop of water and, from that humble beginning, flows into the sea. The current toward a century of human rights has just begun.

The Change Must Start From the People, Not the Government

To study human rights, we must study philosophy. We must study Buddhism. And just as important as studying philosophy is the willingness to stand up for our beliefs and take action. Human rights will never be won unless we speak out, unless we fight to secure them.

Even if human rights are protected and guaranteed by law and government policy, ceaseless efforts are necessary to ensure that they are indeed upheld. Otherwise those rights will become empty, real in theory only.

Why is this? Power is a demonic force that despises human rights, whether it be power of national governments or any other institutions or organizations. Securing human rights protects the individual, based on the awareness that each person is precious, irreplaceable. The purpose of upholding human rights is to enable all people to live with dignity and realize their potential.

Power, instead, looks on people as a mass, not as individuals. It treats them as objects, numbers, statistics.

The SGI fundamentally seeks to transform this thinking. Ours is a struggle for human rights that values each individual.

The SGI's Movement Is a Human Rights Struggle

The Soka Gakkai's movement is a human rights struggle—by the people, for the people. Our movement's history is one of extending a helping hand to those suffering, those lost and forgotten—to people exhausted by sickness and poverty; people devastated by destructive relationships; people alienated and forlorn as a result of family discord or broken homes. We have shared people's sufferings and risen together with them.

Many of your parents have devoted their lives to this struggle for humanity. Desiring neither fame nor status, they strive with a selfless love for humanity, for the benefit of all. They live in the muddy pond of this perverse society but hold a beautiful, pristine ideal above it. They are noble men and women.

I hope you will inherit their commitment and continue to send a great tide of love for humanity around the globe.

How Do I Become a Person of Character, Someone Who Can Protect Human Rights in Society?

You can start by reading good literature. You will find many human rights issues explored in the pages of such works.

You can also learn to recognize the positive qualities in others. One of the first steps in achieving human rights is appreciating and embracing individuality.

It's also important to develop a solid perspective about humanity, realizing that though others may be different from you, we are all members of the same human family. According to

one scientist, ability to differentiate operates at a very shallow level of the brain, while ability to find commonalities involves highly sophisticated information-processing—a much deeper level of the brain.

Those who can get along with all kinds of people, seeing them as equals, as fellow human beings, manifest the true excellence of their character. They are people of genuine culture and education.

Your mission is to make the sun of human rights rise over the twenty-first century. To do that, you must make the courageous sun of love for humanity rise first in your own hearts.

> Transformation in a democratic society does not begin with a strong, charismatic leader. Rather, it begins with the fierce determination of the people to transform their reality.
>
> **Vincent Harding**
> 1931–2014
> Historian, Civil Rights Activist

Notes

1. Translated from German. *Goethes gespräche: Gesamtausgabe* (Goethe's Conversations: Complete Compilation), comp. by Woldemar Frhr. von Biedermann, ed. by Flodoard Frhr. von Biedermann (Leipzig: F. W. v. Biedermann, 1910), vol. 3, 282.

2. Eleanor Roosevelt, *You Learn by Living* (Philadelphia: Westminster Press, 1960), 31–32.

3. Ibid., 32.

4. Michael Barrier, *The Animated Man: A Life of Walt Disney* (Berkeley, CA: University of California Press, 2008), 39.

5. Friedrich von Schiller, *On the Aesthetic Education of Man*, trans. Reginald Snell (London: Routledge & Kegan Paul Ltd., 1957), 120.

6. Antoine de Saint-Exupéry, *Wind, Sand and Stars*, trans. Lewis Galantière (San Diego: Harcourt, Brace & Company, 1939), 215.

7. SGI-USA future division includes members of the elementary and junior high and high school divisions.

8. Rabindranath Tagore, *Thoughts from Rabindranath Tagore* (London: Macmillan and Co., Ltd., 1929), 60.

9. From "Oko Kikigaki" (The Recorded Lectures); not included in *The Writings of Nichiren Daishonin*, vols. 1 and 2.

10. Benedict de Spinoza, *Political Treatise*, http://www.constitution.org/bs/poltr_05.htm.

11. Victor Hugo, *The History of a Crime*, trans. T.H. Joyce and Arthur Locker (New York: Mondial, 2005), 409.

12. Mohandas K. Gandhi, *Gandhi on Non-violence: Selected Texts From Mohandas K. Gandhi's Non-violence in Peace and War*, ed. Thomas Merton (New York: Lee & Low Books, Inc., 1996), 52.

13. Rosa Parks with Gregory J. Reed, *Quiet Strength: The Faith, the Hope and the Heart of a Woman Who Changed a Nation* (Grand Rapids, MI: Zondervan Publishing House, 1994), 72.

Glossary

absolute happiness

> A state of life characterized by a powerful life force and rich wisdom that enables us to overcome any kind of suffering and adversity—a state of being in which living itself is a joy. Attaining absolute happiness is a fundamental goal for all. In contrast, relative happiness comes from fulfilling the endless desires of life, such as wealth, social standing, health, love, etc. Such relative happiness doesn't last long, as it is human nature to always want more.

bodhisattva

> A state of life characterized by compassion, in which one seeks enlightenment for both oneself and others. In this state, one finds satisfaction in devoting oneself to relieving the sufferings of others and leading them to happiness.

Buddha

> One enlightened to the eternal and ultimate truth that is the reality of all things and who leads others to attain the same enlightenment. Nichiren Buddhism, based on the Lotus Sutra, recognizes the potential of every person to become a Buddha.

Buddhahood

> The state of awakening that a Buddha has attained and the ultimate goal of Buddhist practice. The word enlightenment is often used synonymously with Buddhahood. This state of life is characterized by boundless wisdom and infinite compassion. The Lotus Sutra reveals that Buddhahood is a potential in the lives of all living beings.

enlightenment

> See Buddhahood.

faith

A basic attitude in Buddhism, meaning confidence or a belief based on understanding. In Nichiren Buddhism, faith means to believe in the Gohonzon. Faith gives rise to practice and study, and practice and study serve to deepen faith.

Gohonzon

The object of fundamental respect or devotion in Nichiren Buddhism, which expresses the life state of Buddhahood, which all people inherently possess. Chanting Nam-myoho-renge-kyo to it enables us to call forth our own Buddhahood from within.

karma

Potentials in the inner, unconscious realm of life created through one's actions in the past or present that manifest themselves as various results in the present or future. Karma is created through thoughts, words, or deeds. Nichiren Buddhism teaches that karma can be transformed through overcoming delusions, taking action, and above all, chanting Nam-myoho-renge-kyo.

kosen-rufu

Literally, to "widely declare and spread." Nichiren defines Nam-myoho-renge-kyo as the Law to be widely declared and spread. Kosen-rufu refers to the process of securing lasting peace and happiness for all humankind by establishing the humanistic ideals of Nichiren Buddhism in society.

Lotus Sutra

One of the most revered Buddhist scriptures in the world, the Lotus Sutra teaches that all people are potential Buddhas. Nichiren identified the essence of the Lotus Sutra as Nam-myoho-renge-kyo.

major world system

A concept from ancient Indian cosmology, a major world system comprises one billion worlds. The universe was conceived of containing countless major world systems. Today, it could be considered on the scale of a galaxy.

Mystic Law

Also wonderful Law. The ultimate Law, principle, or truth of life and the universe, a translation of *myoho*.

Nam-myoho-renge-kyo

The ultimate Law or truth of the universe that permeates all phenomena. Nichiren established the practice of chanting Nam-myoho-renge-kyo as a means to awaken our Buddhahood. Myoho-renge-kyo is the Japanese reading of the title of the Lotus Sutra, and *nam* means "devotion."

Nichiren (1222–82)

The founder of the Buddhist tradition based on the Lotus Sutra that urges the chanting of Nam-myoho-renge-kyo. Nichiren lived in a time of great conflict and upheaval, and he deeply cared about the suffering of the people. Searching for a way to overcome this suffering, he realized that the Lotus Sutra was the teaching that could help people become happy and bring about peace. Nichiren spread this message and was met with fierce opposition from religious and secular leaders. Undaunted, he lived out his life helping people overcome their problems and laying a firm foundation for the eventual worldwide spread of Nam-myoho-renge-kyo, a legacy embraced by the Soka Gakkai International today.

Soka Gakkai

"Value Creation Society." A lay Buddhist association founded in Japan on November 18, 1930, by Tsunesaburo Makiguchi (1871–1944), its first president, and Josei Toda (1900–58), later its second. Inheriting the legacy of Nichiren, the Soka Gakkai—under its third president, Daisaku Ikeda—has been endeavoring to establish the sanctity of life and the dignity of humanity as fundamental universal ideals. It encourages Buddhist practice as a means for people to develop the character, wisdom, and strength to improve themselves and their circumstances, to contribute to society, and to help bring about happiness and peace in the world.

three thousand realms in a single moment of life

The principle that explains the deep interrelationship of our lives and all phenomena at each moment. Thus, it explains that a change in our inner life exerts an influence on all things and brings about a change in our environment or circumstances, ultimately transforming the world itself.

value creation

The translation of the word *soka* of Soka Gakkai. Value points to the positive aspects of reality that we bring forth when we creatively engage with daily challenges. Value, in this sense, is not something that exists outside us, nor is it a set of criteria for judging behavior. We create value at each moment through our responses to our environment. Depending on our determination, the value created from any situation can be positive or negative, minimal or infinitely great.

Citations for the Nichiren Sidebars